Pointed Sermon Outlines and Illustrations

Pointed Sermon Outlines and Illustrations

By
HYMAN J. APPELMAN

ZONDERVAN PUBLISHING HOUSE
Grand Rapids, Michigan

CONTENTS

1

CHRIST AND THE FALL

Genesis 3:16-19

I. By the Fall
   - A. Pain (vs. 16)
   - B. Subjection (vs. 16)
   - C. The curse (vs. 17)
   - D. Sorrow (vs. 17)
   - E. Thorns (vs. 18)
   - F. Sweat (vs. 19)
   - G. Death (vs. 19)

II. In Christ
   - A. Isa. 53:11 Acts 2:24.
   - B. Gal. 4:4.
   - C. Gal. 3:13.
   - D. Isa. 53:3.
   - E. Matt. 27:29.
   - F. Luke 22:24.
   - G. Phil. 2:8.

* * *

2

THE ARK

Genesis 6:9-22

I. A Memorial of Divine Goodness
   - A. It reminds us of God's saints (I Pet. 3:20).
   - B. It reminds us of God's regard for the families of His saints.
   - C. It reminds us of God's goodness to the world.

II. A Testimony of Noah's Faith
   - A. Built because of Noah's faith.
   - B. Built and furnished by faith.

* * *

3

GOD'S PROVISION FOR THE SINNER'S APPROACH

Leviticus 1:1, 5

I. A PLACE OF MEETING (vs. 1)
Within the sanctuary, at the mercy seat, in the "secret place of the tabernacle of the most High," we may meet Him, "having boldness to enter into the holiest by the blood of Jesus."

II. A SACRIFICIAL BASIS OF ACCEPTANCE
"Through the offering of the body of Jesus Christ once for all" we may approach "in full assurance of faith."

III. A MEDIATORIAL MINISTRY (vs. 5; Heb. 8:1-2; 13:15)
Shall God wait in vain within the Holy Place, and none draw near?
Can sinful man despise the sacrifice of Jesus offered for his propitiation?
With such a priest within the Holy Place, have we no mediation to ask, no sins to confess, no offerings to bring?

* * *

4

THE ANTIDOTE FOR SIN

Leviticus 17:11

I. THE SEVERANCE FROM SIN'S AUTHORITY (Rom. 6:10-11)
II. THE REMOVER OF SIN'S CONDEMNATION (Rom. 8:34)
III. THE MOTIVE FOR ACTION (Rom. 14:15)
IV. THE SEPARATOR FROM SELF'S AGGRANDIZEMENT (II Cor. 5:14, 15—R.V.)
V. THE PROMISE OF COMING GLORY (I Thess. 4:14; 5:10)

* * *

5

THREE REQUISITES FOR REVIVAL

I Samuel 3:21

What wrought the change from emptiness to blessing?

I. A PRAYING MOTHER
II. A CHASTENED PEOPLE
III. A FAITHFUL PROPHET

These three are the beginnings of every great awakening.

* * *

6

THE ROCK

II Samuel 22:32

I. GOD IS A ROCK FOR A—FOUNDATION
Build on it and your house will stand.
II. GOD IS A ROCK FOR A—FORTRESS
Flee to Him to hide.
III. GOD IS A ROCK FOR—SHADE AND REFRESHMENT
Come close to Him out of the scorching heat.

* * *

7

THE STORY OF NAAMAN

II Kings 5

I. THE CURSE (vs. 1)
II. THE COUNSEL (vs. 10)
III. THE CURE (vs. 14)
IV. THE CHURCH RUNNING AFTER THE WORLD'S DOLE (vs. 20)

* * *

8

WHY DO YOU WAIT?

Psalm 39:7

I. YOU DO NOT WAIT BECAUSE YOU ARE SAFE WHILE YOU WAIT
   A. You are condemned already.
   B. The tenure of life is uncertain.
   C. Your character may at any time become fixed in unbelief and love of sin.

II. YOU DO NOT WAIT BECAUSE DELAY MAKES DECISION EASIER

III. YOU DO NOT DELAY BECAUSE THERE IS NOTHING FOR YOU TO DO

* * *

9

SIN TAKES HOLD UPON MEN

Psalm 40:12

I. BY ITS POWER-HABIT

II. BY AN ACCUSING CONSCIENCE

III. BY ITS EVIL CONSEQUENCES
   A. Shame.
   B. Fear.
   C. Punishment.

* * *

10

WHAT WE HAVE IN CHRIST

Psalm 103:4-19

I. FORGIVER (103:5) Isa. 38:17; Isa. 44:22; Jer. 1:20; Micah 7:19; Heb. 10:17; I Pet. 2:24; I John 1:7.

II. HEALER (103:3) Matt. 8:16; Isa. 33:24.
III. REEDEMER (103:4) I Pet. 1:18, 19; Isa. 44:22; Rev. 5:9.
IV. CROWNER (103:4) Lev. 21:12; Isa. 28:5; I Cor. 9:25; I Thess. 2:19; Jas. 1:12; II Tim. 4:8; I Pet. 5:4.
V. SATISFIER (103:5) Isa. 45:2; Ps. 17:15; Ps. 22:26; Ps. 36:8; Ps. 37:19; Ps. 63:5; Ps. 107:9; Isa. 58:11.
VI. PITIER (103:13) Matt. 9:36; 14:14; 20:34; Mark 1:41; Luke 7:13; 10:33; 15:20.
VII. PREPARER OF HIS THRONE (103:19) Luke 19:12; Ps. 72:7, 8.

* * *

11

THE TESTIMONIES OF THE LORD

Psalm 119:2

I. ENLIVENING IN CONTACT (Heb. 4:12)
II. ENLIGHTENING IN OPERATION (Ps. 19:7-8)
III. ENDURING IN SUBSTANCE (I Pet. 1:23)
IV. EMANCIPATING IN MINISTRY (John 8:32)
V. ENNOBLING IN EFFECT (John 17:17)
VI. ENFORCING IN AUTHORITY (Luke 4:32-36; Jer. 23:29)
VII. ENCOURAGING IN PROMISE (II Pet. 1:4)

* * *

12

LIVING

Proverbs 4:23

I. WE MUST HAVE SOMETHING TO LIVE ON
II. WE NEED SOMETHING TO LIVE FOR

III. WE NEED SOMETHING TO LIVE BY
  A. God.
  B. Sincere conviction.
  C. Worthwhile vision.
  D. Noble purpose.
  E. A dominant faith in God.

* * *

13

SEVEN MARVELS OF MERCY

Isaiah 1:18

I. THAT GOD SHOULD FORGIVE AT ALL
He might have dealt with us only according to law and justice.

II. THAT GOD SHOULD BE WILLING TO FORGIVE ALL
"Not willing that any should perish."

III. THAT GOD SHOULD CONDESCEND TO REASON WITH SINNERS

IV. THAT GOD SHOULD OFFER TO REASON WITH US AFTER ALL HE HAS DONE FOR US (Rom. 5:20)

V. THAT GOD SHOULD NOT ONLY FORGIVE BUT TRANSFORM THE SINNER
"As white as snow."
Paul the Saint was Saul the Sinner.

VI. THAT GOD SHOULD FORGIVE AND TRANSFORM ON SUCH EASY TERMS (Isa. 43:25, 26)

VII. THAT GOD SHOULD STILL BEAR PATIENTLY WITH REFUSALS

* * *

14

EXCUSES ANSWERED

Isaiah 1:18

"I intend to be a Christian."

I. BUT I AM TOO GREAT A SINNER (Isa. 1:18)

II. BUT I DO NOT KNOW HOW
- A. Forsake sin (Isa. 55:7; Ps. 66:18, 19).
- B. Believe (John 3:16; 16:31).
- C. Receive (John 1:12).
- D. Acquaint (Job 22:21).
- E. Taste and Trust (Ps. 34:8).

III. BUT I MUST PREPARE MYSELF
- A. Salvation is a gift (Eph. 2:8).
- B. The dying thief (Luke 23:41, 42).

IV. BUT I WANT TO HAVE A GOOD TIME
- A. Rich fool (Luke 12:15-21).
- B. We reap what we sow (Gal. 6:7, 8).

V. BUT I HAVE NOT ENOUGH FEELING
- A. Faith, not feeling, demanded (John 3:36).
- B. Look and live (John 3:14, 15).

VI. BUT I LEAD A MORAL LIFE
- A. None righteous (Rom. 3:10).
- B. Guilt in thought of sin (Matt. 5:28).
- C. Not by works (Tit. 3:5).

VII. BUT NOT TO-NIGHT
- A. Seek now (Isa. 55:6).
- B. Now (II Cor. 6:2).

VIII. BUT THERE ARE SO MANY HYPOCRITES
- A. What is that to thee? (John 21:22, 23).
- B. Look unto Me (Isa. 45:22).

* * *

15

THE ONLY SAFE PLACE

Isaiah 6:1-8

The only safe place in the world is to be where God wants you to be.

I. A VISION OF GOD (vss. 1-4)
II. A VISION OF SELF (vss 5-7)
III. A VISION OF DUTY (vs 8)

* * *

16

THE NAME OF JESUS

Isaiah 9:6-7

I. WONDERFUL OF MARK
II. COUNSELLOR OF MATTHEW
III. MIGHTY GOD OF JOHN
IV. EVERLASTING FATHER OF LUKE
V. PRINCE OF PEACE IN EPISTLES AND REVELATION

* * *

17

THREE WELLS

Isaiah 12:3

I. GOD'S LOVE
II. CHRIST'S BLOOD
III. SPIRIT'S POWER

* * *

18

THE WAY TO HEAVEN

Isaiah 35:8-10

I. A Highway
II. A Holy Way
III. A Plain Way
IV. A Safe Way
V. A Happy Way
VI. A Raised Way
VII. A Simple Way

* * *

19

THE USES OF AFFLICTION

Isaiah 38:16

I. Affliction Teaches Us Our Entire Dependence on God
II. Affliction Disrobes Us of Self-righteousness
III. Affliction Brings Us to Realize and Enjoy the Fullness of Christ
IV. Affliction Stimulates Us in Christian Work

* * *

20

GOD IS

Isaiah 41:10

I. Near to Help
II. Able to Help
III. Willing to Help
IV. Kind in Helping

* * *

21

THE WORK OF FREE GRACE

Isaiah 43:25

Free grace blots out our transgressions:

I. From God's Book

II. With God's Hand

III. For God's Sake

IV. From God's Memory

* * *

22

SALVATION

Isaiah 45:17

I. It Is a Simple Salvation
   - A. Plain.
   - B. Clear.
   - C. Distinct.
   - D. Intelligible in its terms.

II. It Is a Free Salvation
   - A. Unencumbered and unconditional in its offers.
   - B. No costly, protracted, elaborate preparation or probation needed.
   - C. No painful penances, no rites, no fastings, no lustrations, no priestly absolutions (Naaman in Jordan).

III. It Is a Righteous Salvation (vss. 19, 21; Rom. 3:26).

IV. It Is a Sure Salvation (vss. 17, 19, 23)

V. It Is the Only Salvation (vs. 24).

VI. It Is an Eternal Salvation (vs. 17).

* * *

23

CHARACTERISTICS OF AN EFFECTIVE SERVANT OF GOD

Isaiah 50:4, 5

I. Learned Tongue

II. Listening Ear

III. Obedient Life

* * *

24

FALSE RELIGIONS

Isaiah 50:11

I. Man Creates Them—"Ye have kindled the fires"
  A. The religion of creed.
  B. The religion of moods.
  C. The religion of ordinances.
  D. The religion of proxyism—services, priests.
  E. The religion of merit.

II. Heaven Allows Them—"Walk in the light . . ."
  A. The permission is strange.
  B. The permission is significant—shows God's respect for freedom of will.
  C. In giving the Gospel, God has given all that is necessary for man to know to obtain salvation.

III. Misery Follows Them—"This . . . hands"
  A. There is the sorrow of bitter disappointment.
  B. There is the sorrow of poignant remorse.
  C. There is the sorrow of black despair.

* * *

25

WHAT SIN DOES

Isaiah 59:1, 2

I. SIN UNFITS MAN FOR COMMUNION WITH GOD
Unrepented, unforsaken, unforgiven.

II. SIN DISINCLINES MAN FOR COMMUNION WITH GOD
It is enmity against God.

III. SIN EXCLUDES MAN FROM COMMUNION WITH GOD
Sin not only separates us from God, but also God from us.

IV. THE BREACH CAN BE REPAIRED ONLY THROUGH THE MEDIATOR, CHRIST

* * *

26

"THY LIGHT IS COME"

Isaiah 60:1-3

I. THE FACT — Darkness and Light
   A. The darkness of ignorance, of sorrow, of sin.
   B. The light of Christ.

II. THE SUMMONS TO THE CHURCH — "Shine . . . Come"
   A. The silent witness of a Christian life.
   B. Vocal proclamation of His Name.
   C. If we are light, we shall be able to shine.
   D. If we are light, we are bound to shine.
   E. If we are light, we shall wish to shine.

III. THE CONFIDENT PROMISE — "Gentiles . . . rising"
   A. If we have the light, we shall be light.
   B. If we are light, we shall shine.
   C. If we shine, we shall attract.

* * *

27

THE EMBLEMS OF THE SPIRIT

Isaiah 64:12-14

I. WATER — cleansing and fertilizing, refreshing, abundant, freely given

II. FIRE — purifying, illuminating, searching

III. WIND — independent, powerful, sensible in its effects, reviving

IV. OIL — healing, comforting, illuminating, consecrating

V. RAIN AND DEW — fertilizing, refreshing, abundant, imperceptible, penetrating

VI. A DOVE — gentle, meek, innocent, forgiving

VII. A VOICE — speaking, guiding, warning, teaching

VIII. A SEAL — impressing, securing, authenticating

* * *

28

THE INGRATITUDE OF SIN

Jeremiah 2:5-7

I. SEEN IN THE FORGETFULNESS OF GOD'S SAVING MERCY (verse 6)

II. SEEN IN THE IGNORING OF THE PRESENT GOODNESS OF GOD (verse 7)

III. SEEN IN THE FALSE CHARACTER WHICH IS ASCRIBED TO GOD

IV. SEEN IN THE CHARACTER OF THE GODS WHO ARE PREFERRED TO JEHOVAH

V. SEEN IN THE ABUSE AND THE CORRUPTION OF GOD'S GIFTS

* * *

29

THE SINNER

Jeremiah 2:13

I. A SINNER'S LIFE IS LABORIOUS

Sin is toilsome, thankless drudgery.

Sin is a universal deceiver — a cruel, remorseless taskmaster.

II. A SINNER'S WORK IS WORTHLESS

Power, money, glory, fame — all are broken cisterns.

III. A SINNER'S STATE IS APPALLING

Blindness and madness are the results of sin.

IV. A SINNER'S CONDITION IS NOT HOPELESS

God is still the Fountain of living water.

* * *

30

GOD'S USE OF SIN

Jeremiah 2:19

I. GOD USES SIN TO PUNISH SIN

Assyria was used to punish Israel.

II. GOD USES SIN TO DEFEAT SIN

Both were defeated.

III. GOD USES SIN TO REPROVE SIN

IV. GOD USES SIN TO PROMOTE GOODNESS

V. GOD USES SIN TO DISPLAY THE MATCHLESS GLORY OF HIS DIVINE PERFECTIONS

* * *

31

FROM FALSE TO TRUE SALVATION

Jeremiah 3:23

I. THE NEED FOR SALVATION

- A. Universal.
- B. Only God can meet it.

II. THE FALSE HOPE OF SALVATION

- A. Superficially regarded, there was much to recommend the substitute.
  1. It was conspicuous and imposing — on the hilltops.
  2. It was important — judged by noise and bustle.
  3. It was popular — unthinking people go with the multitudes.
  4. It was multiform — sacrifice on every hill.
  5. It was easy to follow — required no purity, no spirituality.
- B. Experience proved the hope to be false.
  1. They were not gods at all.
  2. The corruptions permitted and encouraged proved the nation's ruin.

III. THE TRUE HOPE OF SALVATION

- A. God *only* can deliver.
- B. God *does* deliver by providences in outward events and spiritual help in the internal battle with sin.
- C. God is known as the Deliverer by His actions in the past.
- D. God is sought as the Deliverer when all other refuge fails.

* * *

32

FALSE PEACE

Jeremiah 6:14

I. THE CRAVING FOR PEACE IS NATURAL
   A. Sin is unrest.
   B. Unrest is distressing.

II. THE PRETENSIONS OF FALSE PEACE ARE PLAUSIBLE
   A. They agree with the wishes of the hearers.
   B. They flatter the pride of the populace.
   C. They claim the merits of charity.
   D. They require no sacrifices from those who accept them.
   E. They have appearances in their favor.

III. THE PRETENSIONS OF FALSE PEACE ARE RUINOUS
   A. They do nothing to secure the peace.
   B. They only aggravate the danger.
   C. The nature of the case is misunderstood.

IV. THERE IS A WAY BY WHICH THE NATURAL CRAVING FOR PEACE MAY BE SATISFIED
   A. This is shown to be not immediate.
   B. People must suffer before they enjoy peace through repentance and renewal of life.
   C. There is the fruitless way of reckless transgression, of thoughtlessness and indifference, of base avarice, of exclusive devotion to earthly ambitions, of mere virtuous respectability, of religious indecision.

* * *

33

STRANGE CHURCH-GOERS

Jeremiah 7:9, 10

I. THEY GO TO CHURCH —
   A. For a cloak to cover up their real character.
   B. To pay tribute to the demands of society.
   C. To quiet their conscience.
   D. To set an example.
   E. To propitiate divine favor and secure heaven by and by.

* * *

34

SIN'S RECORD

Jeremiah 17:1

I. SIN LEAVES A RECORD OF ITSELF
II. IT BEGETS CONSEQUENCES, PLANTS MEMORIES, CREATES GUILT
III. THE RECORD IS INEFFACEABLE, INDELIBLE
   A. Useless to ignore it.
   B. Vain to try to wash it away by any effort of our own.
   C. Foolish to expect peace with God until this terrible hindrance has been removed out of the way.

* * *

35

THE PEOPLE'S CHOICE

Jeremiah 21:8-10

I. THE CHOICE WAS FREE
II. THE CHOICE WAS MOMENTOUS

III. THE CHOICE WAS LIMITED

IV. THE CHOICE OF LIFE INVOLVED SAFETY WITH SUBMISSION

* * *

36

THE EVERLASTING LOVE OF GOD

Jeremiah 31:3

I. THE WONDER OF THE FACT
   - A. Our unworthiness.
   - B. Our indifference.
   - C. Our unfaithfulness.

II. SOME REASONS WHY GOD'S LOVE IS EVERLASTING
   - A. The nature of God — "God is love."
   - B. God's relations with us — God is our Father.
     A Parent's love is not caused or limited by the merits of his children.

III. THE PRACTICAL CONSEQUENCES THAT FLOW FROM THE EVERLASTING LOVE
   - A. God will do all that is possible for our highest good.
   - B. We should return to Him with trust and love.
     1. Repent and no longer abuse His goodness.
     2. Trust in Him. Love Him in return for His love.
     3. Find our rest and joy in Him.
     4. Devote ourselves to His service.
     5. Love our brethren with Godlike love for the sake of God's love (I John 4:11).

* * *

37

AN URGENT PRAYER

Jeremiah 31:7

I. INVOLVES THE IDEA OF PERIL
 A. Of worldly conformity.
 B. Of spiritual apathy.
 C. Of sordid selfishness.
 D. Of sectarian divisions.

II. WHAT THE TEXT INCLUDES
 A. A *conviction* of our perilous state.
 B. An earnest longing for the Church's revival and prosperity.
 C. A confident persuasion that God will hear us.

III. THE GROUNDS ON WHICH WE SHOULD EARNESTLY PRESENT THIS PRAYER
 A. From a deep concern for the glory of Christ.
 B. For the well-being of mankind.
 C. Because our own spiritual prosperity is intimately and inseparably connected with it.

* * *

38

BUILDING ON SAND

JEREMIAH 43:8-13

Who builds on sand?

I. THOSE THAT THINK TO ESTABLISH THEMSELVES BY WICKED WAYS

II. THOSE THAT RELY UPON MEN AND NOT ON GOD

III. THOSE THAT TRUST TO UNCERTAIN RICHES

IV. THOSE WHO THINK THAT SAYING "LORD, LORD," WHILE THEY CONTINUE TO LIVE UNGODLY LIVES WILL SAVE THEM

* * *

39

A DOOR OF HOPE

Hosea 2:14, 15

I. THE TROUBLE WHICH DETACHES US FROM EARTH GIVES US NEW HOPE

II. THAT WHICH UNITES US TO GOD GIVES US NEW HOPE

III. THAT WHICH WE BEAR RIGHTLY, WITH GOD'S HELP, GIVES US NEW HOPE

IV. "TRIBULATION WORKETH PATIENCE; AND PATIENCE, EXPERIENCE; AND EXPERIENCE, HOPE"

* * *

40

"WHAT WILL YE DO?"

Hosea 9:5

I. WHAT WILL YE DO WHEN EARTHLY PLANS AND PLEASURES FAIL?

   A. When abandoned by earthly friends?

   B. When religious observances are found to be empty forms?

   C. When death and judgment come?

II. THE SOLEMN DAYS OF LIFE

   A. The day of affliction.

   B. The day of death.

   C. The day of social bereavement.

   D. The day of judgment.

* * *

41

THE DIVIDED HEART

Hosea 10:2

I. A FEARFUL DISEASE
- A. Vital.
- B. Deadly.
- C. Loathsome.
- D. Hard to cure.
- E. Chronic.

II. USUAL SYMPTOMS
- A. Formality.
- B. Inconsistency.
- C. Variableness in object.
- D. Frivolity in religion.

III. SAD EFFECTS
- A. Makes one unhappy.
- B. Makes one useless in the Church.
- C. Makes one dangerous to the world.
- D. Makes one a reprobate in the sight of God.

IV. FUTURE CONSEQUENCES
- A. Outward prosperity used for selfish ends.
- B. Self considered the source, the end (Zech. 7:6).
- C. Outward prosperity used in disregard of God.
- D. Divided allegiance (II Kings 17:32).
- E. Forms of devotion in proportion to outward prosperity.
- F. Outward prosperity abused will bring punishment.

* * *

42

SOWING TO RIGHTEOUSNESS

Hosea 10:12

I. A PRESENT DUTY
- A. Fallow ground must be broken up.
- B. Proper seed must be sown — with intelligence and diligence.
- C. God must be sought — diligently, earnestly, persistently.

II. AN URGENT REASON
- A. The Scriptures urge it.
- B. Common observation urges it.
- C. Past experience urges it.

III. A BLESSED RESULT
- A. If sinners seek the Lord, He will be found.
- B. If they sow in righteous works, they shall reap in mercy.
- C. If they turn from sin, divine blessings shall be given in rich abundance.

* * *

43

CHRIST'S MISSION

Matthew 1:21

I. CHRIST'S MAIN MISSION IS TO SAVE SINNERS
- A. The great evil from which Christ saves is sin.
- B. The salvation is for Christ's people.
  1. God the Father *with* us at Bethlehem.
  2. God the Son *for* us at Calvary.
  3. God the Holy Spirit *in* us at Pentecost.
- C. An omnipotent Saviour.

D. A willing Saviour.
E. A living Saviour.
F. A present Saviour.
G. A personal Saviour.
H. A sympathizing Saviour.

* * *

44

THE CHRISTIAN'S CROSS

MATTHEW 10:38

I. EVERY CHRISTIAN HAS HIS CROSS
II. EVERY CHRISTIAN IS REVEALED BY THE WAY IN WHICH HE DEALS WITH HIS CROSS
  A. He may spurn it.
  B. He may leave it.
  C. He may lift it.
  D. He is disloyal if he spurns it.
  E. He is negligent if he leaves it.
  F. He is truehearted if he lifts it.

* * *

45

THE POWER OF CHRISTIANITY

Matthew 13:33, 34

I. CHRISTIANITY IS AN IMPORTED POWER
  A. Not inherent in the world.
  B. Dissimilar in spirit and opposed in aim.
II. IT IS OF DIVINE ORIGIN

III. IT IS A HIDDEN POWER

IV. IT IS A QUIET POWER IN THE HEART

V. IT IS AN ASSIMILATING POWER

A. Makes the lump like itself.

B. Gives men the Spirit of Christ.

VI. IT IS A DIFFUSIVE POWER — "leaveneth the whole lump"

A. Gradually diffusive, from particle to particle.

B. Universally diffusive.

* * *

46

WHY STAND YE HERE ALL THE DAY IDLE?

Matthew 20:6

I. THE VINEYARD IS SO SPACIOUS

II. THE REWARD IS SO LIBERAL

III. THE MASTER IS SO KIND

IV. THE TIME OF WORKING IS SO SHORT

* * *

47

THE JOY THAT JESUS BRINGS

Luke 2:15-20

I. THE INVESTIGATION (verse 15)

A. They went personally — "Let *us* go."

B. They went immediately — "Let us *now* go" (Acts 24:25; II Cor. 6:2).

II. THE CONFIRMATION (verses 16 and 17)

A. The discovery (verse 16).

B. "And they came" — not to the artist, poet, etc., but to the manger (Phil. 2:6-8; Isa. 53:3).

C. The declaration — their testimony (verse 17).

III. THE REVELATION (verse 14).

A. What they had heard (verse 14).

1. Nationally (Isa. 9:16; Rev. 18:11-16).
2. Individually (John 1:11, 12; Rom. 6:1).

B. What they had seen (verses 20, 30).

—*Moody Monthly*

* * *

48

A VISION OF GOD

Luke 2:30

I. GIVEN TO US IN THE BIBLE AS THE CLUE TO ALL THE DEEPER ASPECTS OF LIFE AND THE REMEDY FOR ALL ITS EVILS (e.g., Jacob at Peniel, Gen. 32:30)

II. GIVES CERTAINTY CONCERNING THE CALL OF GOD, AND THE MISSION OF LIFE AS IN THE CASE OF MOSES (Ex. 3:14)

III. GIVES US COURAGE FOR LIFE'S TASKS AND DIFFICULTIES (e.g., Josh. 5:13, 15)

IV. BRINGS REASSURANCE FROM DESPAIR AND CONSOLATION IN LONELINESS (Gen. 16:13, 14; I Kings 19:11-13)

V. GIVES THE TRUEST VISION OF HIMSELF (Job 42:5, 6; Isa. 6:5; Luke 5:8)

* * *

49

THE MIRACULOUS DRAUGHT OF FISHES

Luke 5

I. WHY WE SOMETIMES FAIL
- A. Iniquity.
- B. Indifference.
- C. Inattentiveness.

II. WHAT FAILURE MAY DO TO US
- A. Stop.
- B. Sour.
- C. Save.

III. WHAT WE MUST DO TO SUCCEED
- A. Study the Word.
- B. Seek His face.
- C. Surrender our wills.
- D. Confess.
- E. Consecrate
- F. Concentrate.

* * *

50

MEN OUGHT ALWAYS TO PRAY

Luke 18:1

To neglect prayer is to burden ourselves with care, to shut ourselves out of blessing, to enfeeble our faith, to dim the eyes of our hope, to damp the fire of our zeal, to relax the grip of our tenacity, to weaken the heart of our love and to rob our service of its strength.

I. PRAYER IS A SIN-KILLER

Iniquity in the heart will keep prayers from being answered (Ps. 66:18).

II. PRAYER IS A POWER BRINGER
Pentecost (Acts 1:14; 2:1).

III. PRAYER IS A VICTORY GAINER
Nehemiah won because he made his "prayer unto God" (Neh. 4:9).

IV. PRAYER IS AN OBSTACLE REMOVER
Peter was brought out of prison in answer to prayer (Acts. 12:5).

V. PRAYER IS A HOLINESS PROMOTER
It takes us to God with our need, and brings God with His supply. Pray always and in everything (Eph. 6:18; Phil. 4:6).

VI. PRAYER IS A BLESSING BRINGER
Elijah prayed for rain (Jas. 5:17, 18).

VII. PRAYER IS A BODY HEALER
We are assured "the prayer of faith shall save the sick."

* * *

51

THE SAVIOUR'S MESSAGE FROM THE CROSS

Luke 23

I. IN ITS FERVENT SUPPLICATION (Luke 23:34)
II. IN ITS GRACIOUS FORGIVENESS (Luke 23:43)
III. IN ITS SELF-FORGETFUL SYMPATHY (John 19:26, 27)
IV. IN ITS VICARIOUS SUFFERING (Matt. 27:25-46)
V. IN ITS INTENSE DESIRE (John 19:28*a*)
VI. IN ITS COMPLETE PROVISION (John 19:30)
VII. IN ITS IMPLICIT CONFIDENCE AND VOLUNTARY COMMITTAL (Luke 23:46)

* * *

52

THE ABIDING CHRIST

Luke 24:29

I. THE HIDDEN GUEST

II. THE HUMBLE GUEST

He does not force His way in, nor does He seek a contrived invitation.

III. THE HONORED GUEST

He must be Head. He will not take a corner place.

* * *

53

CHRIST FORSAKEN

JOHN 1:11

I. BY THE WORLD (1:10)

II. BY HIS NATION (1:11)

III. BY HIS COUNTRY

IV. BY HIS CITY (Luke 4:16, 29)

V. BY HIS KINDRED (John 7:5)

VI. BY HIS FRIENDS (Matt. 26:5)

VII. BY HIS GOD (Matt. 26:46)

The Son of God became the Son of Man so that the sons of men might become the sons of God.

* * *

54

THE HOLY SPIRIT IN THE CHRISTIAN LIFE

John 7:37, 38

I. THE PERFECT LIFE LIVED BY OUR LORD AND MASTER WAS LIVED IN THE POWER OF THE HOLY SPIRIT (Matt. 3:11; 4:1; Luke 4:18)

II. THE CHRISTIAN LIFE OF THE NEW TESTAMENT IS A LIFE LIVED IN THE HOLY GHOST

III. EVERY BELIEVER IN CHRIST IS THEN CAPABLE OF LIVING THE CHRIST-LIFE IN ALL ITS FULLNESS

IV. THE MOMENT WE BELIEVE IN CHRIST WE RECEIVE THE HOLY SPIRIT.

V. THE HOLY SPIRIT TEACHES US TO PRAY (Rom. 8:26) AND ILLUMINES OUR MINDS (Rom. 16:13)

* * *

55

THE LOVE OF CHRIST

John 13:1

I. EXTERNAL (Prov. 8:22-31)

II. INFINITE (John 15:9)

III. UNMERITED (Rom. 5:8)

IV. UNCHANGING (John 13:1)

V. INSEPARABLE (Rom. 8:35-39)

VI. PERFECT (I John 4:17)

VII. CONSTRAINING (II Cor. 5:14)

* * *

56

THE COST OF PENTECOST

Acts 2:1

I. WHAT IT COST GOD IN JESUS CHRIST: A CROSS (Isa. 53:3-10; Phil. 2:5-11; Heb. 2:9, 10; 5:7-9)

II. WHAT IT COST THE DISCIPLES: A CROSS (II Cor. 11:23-28; Gal. 2:20; 6:14; Phil. 3:4-14)

III. WHAT IT COSTS US: A CROSS (Luke 14:25-27; Heb. 11:32; 12:4; Rom. 6:6-8; 12:1, 2; Gal. 5:24; Luke 9:23)

* * *

57

WORK FOR CHRIST

Acts 9:6

I. The Field Is Large (Matt. 13:38)
II. The Need Is Great (John 4:35)
III. The Time Is Now (Gal. 6:10)
IV. The Call Is Urgent (Matt. 20:6)
V. The Work Is Varied (Matt. 13:34)
VI. The Partner Is Almighty (II Cor. 6:1)
VII. The Means Are Provided (Luke 19:15)
VIII. The Reward Is Sure (Dan. 12:3)

* * *

58

THREE KINDS OF HEARERS

Acts 17:32-34

I. Those Who Hear and Work
  A. When they hear and fear.
  B. When they cannot confute nor silence.
  C. When they do not understand or try to understand.
  D. When they weigh the risk of yielding.
II. Those Who Hear and Procrastinate
  A. Almost persuaded.
  B. Have neither an honest nor an earnest heart.
III. Those Who Hear and Believe
  A. The Lord opens their hearts.
  B. They feel that the truth is for them.
  C. They are ready to forsake all and cleave to the Lord.

* * *

59

PAUL THE SLAVE

Romans 1:1

I. A SLAVE TO TRUTH
  A. The books of Romans (Rom. 5) and Galatians.
  B. Paul opposed falsehood and paid for it.
  C. Other early Christians — Luther, Bunyan and Wesley — also paid for their opposition to falsehood.
  D. There is opposition to truth today.

II. A SLAVE TO LOVE
  A. The greatest constraint in the world (II Cor. 5:14, 15 and Phil 3:7-11).

III. A SLAVE TO COMPASSION (Rom. 9:1 and I Cor. 9:19-23)

* * *

60

THE GREAT THEME

Romans 2:2

I. REDEMPTION IS BY CHRIST CRUCIFIED (Eph. 1:7; I Pet. 1:10; Gal. 3:13; Col. 1:14; Rev. 5:9)

II. PEACE OF CONSCIENCE COMES THROUGH CHRIST CRUCIFIED (Col. 1:20)

III. DEATH TO SIN COMES THROUGH CHRIST CRUCIFIED (Gal. 2:20; 6:14)

IV. THE SUPREME ARGUMENT OF LOVE IS IN CHRIST CRUCIFIED (Eph. 5:2)

V. THE SUPREME EXAMPLE OF PATIENCE IS IN CHRIST CRUCIFIED (I Pet. 2:20-24)

VI. ENMITY TO HIS CROSS IS A FATAL SIN (Heb. 10:29 Phil. 2:18, 19)

* * *

61

REDEMPTION

Romans 3:24

I. THE SUBJECTS OF REDEMPTION
   Those who were in bondage to a "vain manner of living" (I Pet. 1:18).
II. THE SOURCE OF REDEMPTION (Rom. 3:24; Eph. 1:7)
III. THE PRICE OF REDEMPTION
   His blood (Eph. 1:7; Matt. 20:28; I Tim. 2:6).
IV. THE SUBSTANCE OF REDEMPTION
   Christ is its substance and embodiment (I Cor. 1:30).
V. THE RECEIVER OF REDEMPTION
   Faith.
VI. THE MEANING OF REDEMPTION
   Deliverance.
VII. THE CONSUMMATION OF REDEMPTION
   Our Lord's return (Rom. 8:23).

* * *

62

GOD'S FELLOW WORKERS

I Corinthians 3:9

This is the noblest conception of life voiced in the Scripture.

I. WE MUST BEGIN BY REALIZING THAT GOD HAS A PURPOSE IN OUR LIVES, THAT HE HAS PUT US HERE FOR A GOOD PURPOSE
II. WE MUST PROCEED BY DEDICATING OUR LIVES TO HIM, PUTTING ALL THAT WE ARE AT HIS DISPOSAL

III. WE MUST CONTINUE BY FOLLOWING THE LEADERSHIP AND EXAMPLE OF JESUS

IV. WE MUST REMEMBER THAT IF WE WORK WITH GOD, GOD WORKS WITH US, (Mark 16:20) GUARANTEEING SUCCESS AND ASSURING US OF RICH REWARDS

* * *

63

OF WHAT IMPORTANCE IS THE EMPTY TOMB?

I Corinthians 15:12-19

I. ON CHRIST'S RESURRECTION THE AUTHENTICITY OF THE BIBLE STANDS OR FALLS
   A. The Old Testament predicted it (Ps. 16:8-10).
   B. Christ predicted it (Matt. 20:17-19).
   C. The disciples testified concerning it (Acts 1:2, 3).
   D. Paul testified concerning it (I Cor. 15:8).

II. CHRIST'S RESURRECTION IS PROOF OF HIS DEITY
   A. It proved Him to be the Son of God (Rom. 1:4).
   B. It proved His claims regarding Himself (John 10:18).
   C. It shows that God accepted Him and His work (Eph. 1:19, 20).

III. CHRIST'S RESURRECTION IS THE GROUND OF OUR STANDING AND STATE
   A. It gives assurance of eternal life (I Pet. 1:3-5).
   B. It shows that believers are "justly justified" (Rom. 4:25).
   C. It gives believers an accepted Intercessor (Rom. 8:34).
   D. It secures the believer's resurrection (I Cor. 15:21, 22; Rom. 8:11).

—ROBERT K. KINNEY

* * *

64

THE GREAT SACRIFICE

II Corinthians 8:9

I. HE WAS RICH

  A. He shared the glory of the infinite God, eternal, immortal, invisible.

  B. He possessed the love of the Father.

  C. He had the service and fellowship of all the heavenly hosts.

  D. He was the Creator, and therefore the Owner of the entire universe with all its wealth.

II. HE BECAME POOR

  A. He suffered poverty beyond compare.

  B. He had nowhere to lay His head.

  C. He walked, He toiled, He hungered, He wept.

* * *

65

THE JUSTIFIED LIFE

Galatians 2:16-20

I. JUSTIFIED

  A. Not by works (Eph. 2:1-12; Titus 3:3-7).

  B. By the grace of God (Rom. 3:20-26).

  C. Through faith in Christ (Rom. 5:1, 2).

  D. Faithfully.

  E. Fully.

  F. Freely.

II. CRUCIFIED

  A. Changed (II Cor. 5:17).

  B. Consecrated (Rom. 12:1, 2).

  C. Concentrated (Heb. 12:1-4).

III. VIVIFIED
   A. Emancipated (John 8:30-36).
   B. Enlightened (John 16:12, 13).
   C. Empowered (Acts 2:38-40).

* * *

66

LIVING YOUR RELIGION

Galatians 6:2, 7-9, 14

I. BEAR
   A. Your own burdens, common, as a Christian (Jas. 1:2-4).
      1. Do not bewail.
      2. Do not compromise.
      3. Do not shirk.
   B. The other fellow's burdens.
      1. Gainlessly.
      2. Sacrificially.
      3. Unenvyingly (Exod. 32:30).

II. SOW
   A. Constantly.
      1. Each gesture.
      2. Each word.
      3. Each thought.
      4. Each act.
   B. Consistently.
      1. With your profession.
      2. With needs about you.
      3. With opportunities.
   C. Conscientiously.
      1. With an eye to Christ's glory.
      2. With an eye to helping others.
      3. With an eye to eternal results.

III. GLORY

A. In the Cross.

1. Naught else.
2. No one else.

* * *

67

PRAISE FOR THE WORK OF THE TRINITY IN THE GOSPEL OF GRACE

Ephesians 1:14

I. THE GRACE OF CHRIST ORIGINATED IN THE LOVE OF THE FATHER

A. He has chosen us to holiness (verses 3, 4).

B. He has ordained us to sonship (verse 5).

C. He has accepted us in Christ (verse 6).

II. THE GRACE OF CHRIST WAS WROUGHT OUT BY THE SUFFERINGS OF THE SON

A. In Him we have forgiveness of sins.

B. In Him we have the revelation of the mystery of the divine will (verses 8, 9).

C. In Him we enjoy the unity and grandeur of the heavenly inheritance (verses 10-12).

III. THE GRACE OF CHRIST IS CONFIRMED AND REALIZED BY THE OPERATION OF THE HOLY SPIRIT

A. By it we hear and understand the Word of Truth (verse 13).

B. It is an earnest of our possessing the full inheritance of blessing (verses 13, 14).

* * *

68

COURSE OF SPIRITUAL COMMUNION

Phillipians 3

I. A CONSCIOUS DISSATISFACTION WITH THE PRESENT

A. St. Paul with his might in the race.

II. A COMPARATIVE OBLIVIOUSNESS TO THE PAST

A. St. Paul with his back to the past — what a past —!

III. A CONCENTRATED STRUGGLE FOR THE FUTURE

A. St. Paul with his eye on the goal, Jesus Christ.

* * *

69

THE CHRISTIAN'S STRENGTH

Philippians 4

I. THE SPHERE OF A CHRISTIAN'S ABILITY

A. Able to undergo every trial.

B. Able to brave every sort of suffering.

C. Able to overcome every variety of temptation.

D. Able to perform every sort of duty.

II. THE SOURCE OF THE CHRISTIAN'S STRENGTH

A. By Christ's teaching.

B. By His example of holy patience and forbearance.

C. By the moral influence of His death as a real sacrifice for sin.

D. By the abundant bestowal of His Holy Spirit.

* * *

70

CHRIST IS ALL

Colossians 3:11

I. CHRIST IS ALL IN SALVATION

A. Died to save us from the penalty and guilt of sin.

B. Lives to deliver from the power and government of sin.

C. He is coming again to emancipate from the presence of sin.

II. CHRIST IS ALL IN SANCTIFICATION

A. The *cause* of our sanctification is the Father.

B. The *agent,* the Holy Spirit.

C. The *ground,* the Atonement of Christ.

D. The *measure,* the Person and position of Christ.

E. Manifestation of Christ (Gal. 2:20; Phil. 1:21; John 15:4).

III. CHRIST IS ALL IN SERVICE

A. He is the *motive.*

B. He is the *method.*

C. In Him is the *might.*

* * *

71

WITNESSING

I Thessalonians 1:8

I. THE BLIND MAN WITNESSED TO CHRIST'S SIGHT-GIVING POWER (John 9:25)

II. THE DEMONIAC WITNESSED TO CHRIST'S DELIVERING GRACE (Mark 5:20)

III. THE LEPER WITNESSED TO CHRIST'S CLEANSING TOUCH (Mark 1:45)

IV. THE WOMEN WITNESSED TO CHIST'S SATISFYING LOVE (Luke 7:37)

V. THE CROOKED WOMEN WITNESSED TO CHRIST'S STRAIGHTENING MIGHT (Luke 13:13)

VI. THE RAISED MAN WITNESSED TO CHRIST'S QUICKENING LIFE (Luke 7:15)

VII. THE DISCIPLES WITNESSED TO CHRIST'S EXCELLENT GLORY (John and Luke 14; II Pet. 1:16)

VIII. THE SAINTS AT THESSALONICA WITNESSED TO CHRIST'S EFFECTIVE WORKING (I Thess 1:9, 10)

* * *

72

FIVE GREAT THINGS

Titus 2:11-14

I. A GREAT REVELATION (verse 11)

II. A GREAT OBLIGATION (verse 12)

III. A GREAT INSPIRATION (verse 13)

IV. A GREAT SALVATION (verse 14)

V. CHRIST'S GREAT SELF BESTOWMENT (verse 14)

He gave Himself, the great emancipation, that He might redeem us, the great acquisition, and purify unto Himself a people for a possession, the great possession.

Salvation is based upon Divine mercy. It is independent of human merit and only attainable by a new creation.

* * *

73

CHRIST FOR EVERY MAN

Titus 2:11-14

I. THE GRACE OF GOD
  A. The Grace of God.
  B. The Grace of God that bringeth salvation.
  C. The Grace of God that bringeth salvation has appeared to all men.

II. THE GIVING CHRIST
  A. Who gave Himself.
  B. Who gave Himself for us.
  C. Who gave Himself for us that He might redeem us from all iniquity.

* * *

74

GOD IS ABLE

Hebrews

I. ABLE TO SYMPATHIZE (Heb. 4:15)
II. ABLE TO SUCCOR (Heb 2:18)
III. ABLE TO SAVE (Heb. 7:25)
IV. ABLE TO MAKE YOU STAND (Rom. 14:4)
V. ABLE TO STABLISH YOU (Rom. 16:25)
VI. ABLE TO KEEP YOU FROM FALLING AND TO PRESENT YOU FAULTLESS (Jude 24)
VII. ABLE TO MAKE GRACE ABOUND TOWARD YOU (II Cor. 9:8)
VIII. ABLE TO KEEP (II Tim. 1:12)
IX. ABLE TO BUILD YOU UP (Acts 20:32)
X. ABLE EVEN TO SUBDUE YOU (Phil. 3:21)
XI. ABLE TO DO EXCEEDINGLY ABUNDANTLY ABOVE ALL THAT WE ASK OR THINK (Eph. 3:20)

* * *

75

THE LIFE OF FAITH

Hebrews 11

I. THE PURPOSE OF FAITH

To make real the things not seen (verses 1-3).

II. THE PLAN OF FAITH

Righteousness from God through another's death, Christ's sacrifice (verse 4).

III. THE PROGRESS OF FAITH

Coming, believing, seeking, walking, pleasing, translation (verses 5, 6; Gen. 5:24).

IV. THE PREPARATION OF FAITH

Warns of "things not seen as yet" (verse 7).

V. THE PILGRIMAGE OF FAITH

Led of God "not knowing whither," showing obedience (verse 8).

VI. THE PROMISE OF FAITH

"A city," an eternal abiding place (verses 9, 10).

VII. THE POWER OF FAITH

Receives strength for the impossible (verses 11, 12).

VIII. THE PERSUASION OF FAITH

Sees and embraces things promised (verse 13).

IX. THE PROFESSION OF FAITH

Declares with assurance the things promised (verses 13, 14).

X. THE PROSPECT OF FAITH

God, and the things "prepared for them" by Him (verses 15, 16).

XI. THE PRACTICE OF FAITH

In all things, it accounts God able and sufficient (verses 17, 18).

XII. THE PROVISION OF FAITH
Provides blessings for future generations (verses 20-22).

XIII. THE PROTECTION OF FAITH
"Hid", "not afraid", "kept", "passed through" (verses 23-29).

XIV. THE PATIENCE OF FAITH
"Seven days"—obeys to the completeness of God's time (verse 30).

XV. THE PEACE OF FAITH
Lays hold of God amid calamity (verse 31).

XVI. THE PROOFS OF FAITH
Sees God victorious in other lives and other times (verses 32-39).

XVII. THE PERFECTION OF FAITH
The resurrection glory of all the redeemed (verse 40).

XVIII. THE PERSONIFICATION OF FAITH
"Jesus, the author and finisher of our faith" (12:3).

JESSIE V. BENNER in *Moody Monthly*

* * *

76

ASSURANCE

II Peter 1:4

I. GOD'S JUSTICE WILL NOT SUFFER HIM TO DECEIVE
II. GOD'S GRACE WILL NOT SUFFER HIM TO FORGET
III. GOD'S TRUTH WILL NOT SUFFER HIM TO CHANGE
IV. GOD'S POWER WILL NOT SUFFER HIM TO BECOME INCAPABLE OF FULFILLING HIS PROMISES

* * *

77

THE CONQUESTS OF PRAYER

I John 5:14, 15

I. THE CONTENTS
   A. God's work advanced.
   B. God's way chosen.
   C. God's will obeyed.

II. THE CONFIDENCE
   A. God's honor involved.
   B. God's power manifested.
   C. God's glory enhanced.

III. THE CONQUESTS
   A. Satan conquered.
   B. Saints consecrated.
   C. Sinners converted.

* * *

78

THE MEDIATORIAL POWER OF CHRIST

Revelation 3:5

I. SYMBOLIZES THE MEDIATORIAL POWER OF CHRIST
   A. The origin of His mediatorial power.
   B. The nature of His mediatorial power.
   C. The exercise of His mediatorial power.
   D. The extent of His mediatorial power.
   E. Its final end and completion.

II. EXHIBITS THE BASIS ON WHICH THIS MEDIATORIAL POWER RESTS
   A. The Lion of the Tribe of Judah (Gen. 49:9).
      Hence his right was from the office predicted.
   B. The Root of David.
      By descent also, as Heir of Him to whom God's promises of universal rule have been given.

C. The Lamb slain.
The pre-eminent right secured by the Atonement.

III. REVEALS THE RESULTS CONTEMPLATED BY HIS MEDIATORIAL POWER
A. To set forth the glory of the Son of God.
B. To secure the accomplishment of man's redemption.

* * *

79

THE UNIQUENESS OF CHRIST'S BLOOD

Revelation 5:9

I. SUBLIMELY UNIQUE IN ITS NATURE
A. In accordance with eternal plan of God.
B. Voluntary in the sense in which no other man's death is voluntary.
C. Absolutely free from all imperfections.

II. SUBLIMELY UNIQUE IN ITS EFFORTS
A. Variously represented
B. Reconciliation (Atonement).
C. Purifying (Soul Life).
D. Ransom (Conquering Force).
E. Eternal.

III. SUBLIMELY UNIQUE IN ITS AVAILABILITY

* * *

80

KING OF KINGS AND LORD OF LORDS

Revelation 19:16

I. IF CHRIST BE KING OF KINGS AND LORD OF LORDS, THEN WE HAVE CONFIDENCE THAT HE WILL DIRECT

Whatever Pertains To Our Spiritual Interests, So As To Promote and Secure Our Growth In Grace and Our Final Salvation

II. If Christ Be King of Kings and Lord of Lords, Then the Church Is Safe

III. If Christ Be King of Kings and Lord of Lords, Then Individual Christians Are Safe

IV. If Christ Be So Great a King He Ought to Be Feared

V. He Ought to Be Adored

VI. He Ought to Be Obeyed

* * *

Illustrations

BURNING

The spirit of man is the candle of the Lord . . .
(*Proverbs* 20:27)

An unlighted candle stands in the darkness. Here comes someone to light it. A blazing bit of paper holds the fire at first, but it is vague and fitful. It flares and wavers and at any moment may go out. But the vague, uncertain, flaring blaze touches the candle, and the candle catches fire and at once you have a steady flame. It burns straight and clear and constant.

The candle gives the fire a manifestation-point for all the room which is illuminated by it. The candle is glorified by the fire and the fire is manifested by the candle. The two bear witness that they were made for one another by the way in which they fulfill each other's life. That fulfillment comes by the way in which the inferior substance renders obedience to its superior.

The *docile wax* acknowledges that the subtle flame is its master and it yields to his power. *The disobedient granite,* on the other hand, neither gives the fire any chance to show its brightness nor gathers any splendor to itself. It merely glows with sullen resistance, and, as the heat increases, splits and breaks but will not yield.

* * *

CAPTAIN

Two children were standing on the deck of an ocean liner looking out upon the great ocean. "What makes this ship go?" asked the boy of his sister.

"Why, the captain, he makes this ship go," answered the little girl, as she looked up to the bridge on which the captain, bedecked in his gold braid, walked back and forth.

"Oh, no he doesn't," said the boy. "What do girls know about ships anyway? You come with me and I'll show you what makes this big ship go."

So the boy took his sister by the hand and led her down to the engine room where he showed her those gigantic engines, and said to his sister, "See, that's what makes this ship go — not the captain but the engines make it go."

A little later as the boy and his sister were walking the deck again there was a cry, "MAN OVERBOARD!" They looked out to the sea and there, struggling in the water, they saw a drowning man. Then all eyes turned toward the captain on the bridge.

The captain called down one of the tubes, "Stop engines!" And the engines stopped. "Reverse engines!" And the engines reversed. "Forward engines!" And the steamer turned in the direction of the drowning man.

"Throw out the lifeline!" The line was thrown to the drowning man. He grasped it and soon was lifted up to the deck in safety.

The little girl turned to her brother and said, "Didn't I tell you that it was the captain that ran this ship?"

* * *

CHALLENGE

1. In the middle ages Robert Bruce, King of Scotland, vowed to make a pilgrimage to Palestine. Seeing he could not make it, he pleaded with Douglas to remove his heart after his death and carry it to the Holy Land.

This heart was encased in a golden vessel and carried by Douglas into the battle with the Moors of Spain. When Douglas saw that he was losing he rose in his saddle, took the heart and flung it far into the ranks of the Moors — saying as he did so, "There goes the heart of Bruce! Who will follow?" Douglas' men rallied and won.

Jesus has flung His Heart into a lost world — saying, "There is the broken bleeding heart of your King — Who will follow?"

2. The testimony of Nature: Tie a rope around your arm, strapping it to your side. Put a stopper in your ear. Put a bandage over your eyes. Keep it there. The time will come when you will have lost all capacity for seeing, when you will have lost all capacity for hearing, when you will have lost the use of your arm. Even so, in the same way, harden your heart, and the time will come when it will become so hard that nothing can soften it.

* * *

CHOICE

In psychology there is what is called a "major choice" — a choice that doesn't have to be made over again every day. Lesser choices fit into it, not it into them.

* * *

COMPASSION

An Armenian girl and her brother had been attacked by Turks in a lane, and while she had escaped by climbing over a wall, her brother had been brutally killed before her eyes. She was a nurse, and later on while nursing in the hospital recognized one of her patients as the Turkish soldier who had murdered her brother. Her first feeling was — *Revenge!* He was terribly ill, just hovering between life and death. The slightest neglect, and he would die. No one would know. His life was absolutely in her hands. But instead of revenge she decided for Christ's sake to forgive him. She fought for his life and won, nursing him back to health.

When he was convalescent, she told him who she was. The Turkish soldier looked at her in astonishment and said, "Then why didn't you let me die, when you had me in your power?"

"I couldn't," answered the girl. "I just couldn't, for I am a Christian and my own Master forgave His enemies who crucified Him. I must do the same, for His sake."

"Well," said the hardened Turk, "if that's what it means to be a Christian, I want to be one."

* * *

COMPASSION

Matthew 9:36

When I was a student in the seminary, one of my professors one day, in a chapel service, told a story of his own experience. He told how, one winter, his seven-year-old girl contracted pneumonia and had reached the point of death. He told of the doctors, specialists, nurses and medicines that were procured in a seemingly hopeless effort to save the child's life. He told how the family physician came out of the child's room one late afternoon and, putting his arm around the father, told him that the child would not live. The father went into the bedroom and sat down by the side of the bed. His wife was on the other side, her face gaunt, her eyes red-rimmed from watching and weeping. The minutes moved along. The child, with the disease traveling to her heart, began to twist and turn, to push and to pull at her covers. The father, realizing that she was in the throes of death, turned to his wife and told her what the doctor had said. The mother began to cry, but the father remonstrated with her.

"This is no time for tears, Mother," he said, "this is time for prayer. Let us pray. God is merciful. He will save our child."

The pair knelt by the bed of their darling. The mother began to pray but broke down in weeping. The father lifted his voice in prayer. Right there in our chapel service that professor repeated his prayer. Never so long as I live will I forget the pathos of that cry.

"Lord," the father prayed, "our hope is in Thee. The doctors can do no more. We can do no more. Our faith and confidence are in Thee. Lord, You can take every penny we have in the world. You can take every bit of property we have on earth. You can take me; you can take my wife; you can take us both, only spare our child."

God heard and answered that prayer. The child is alive today, married to a preacher, with precious, blessed children of her own. Think of it. If that child would have died, by the Word of God, by the blood of Christ, it would have gone on to glory. Only its body and its little life were at stake. Yet the father and mother offered all they were and had for the sparing of their child's life. All about us are men and women and children whose souls are perishing. Should we not be willing to give our property, to give our money, to give ourselves to save them from a burning hell?

* * *

COMMUNION, 1

The president of one of the largest banks in New York City told that after he had served for several years as an office boy in the bank over which he now presides, the president called him into his office one day and said to him, "I want you to come into my office and be with me."

The young man replied: "But what do you want me to do?"

"Never mind that," said the president, "you will learn about that soon. I just want you to be in here with me."

"That was the most memorable moment in my life," said the great banker. "Being with that man made me all I am today."

* * *

COMMUNION, 2

The late Dwight L. Moody was fond of quoting these words: "It remains yet to be seen what God will do in, through and with any man who will thoroughly consecrate himself to His service."

* * *

CREATION, 1

Someone has figured out how many chances to one it would take for the world to have happened by chance, and the figures go round the world thirty-five times. "A preposterous figure," says Dr. Millikan, the scientist.

Sir James Jeans has figured out that it would take a hundred million years for a hundred thousand monkeys, pecking at random on a hundred thousand typewriters, to happen by chance upon the works of Shakespeare. And then, after they had happened upon the arrangement of the letters, they wouldn't know what the letters meant!

* * *

CREATION, 2

A professor of electrical engineering, after passing through agnosticism to faith, put it this way: "If anyone could prove to me scientifically that this thing I have found is not true, I would still have to believe it, for the universe wouldn't make sense without it."

* * *

DEATH, 1

The minister was fond of visiting the sick and the dying because "I like to take a look over the brink."

* * *

DEATH, 2

William the Conqueror established the ringing of curfew bells. The meaning of that curfew bell, sounded at eventime, was that all the fires should be put out or covered with ashes, all the lights extinguished and the people should go to bed. Soon for us the curfew will sound. The fires of our lives will be banked up in ashes, and we shall go to sleep. There is no gloom in that if we are ready. The best thing that a Christian can do is die.

* * *

DEATH, 3

An old slave, when told by his doctor that he was near death, said, "Bless you, Doctor, don't let that bother you; that's what I've been living for."

* * *

DELAY

(*Proverbs.* 29:1)

A French captain was walking along the shore at Dover, England, just walking along and looking out to sea, when suddenly he stumbled and fell to one knee. He noticed that his right foot had caught in the link of a chain, a great cable, an anchor chain rusted with the abandoned years. He started to pull his foot out but it would not come. He twisted it, turned it, kept on turning and twisting.

He was a strong man. The first thing he knew, the foot began to swell. He untied his shoe, thinking he would pull out his stockinged foot. He kept on pulling and straining, tried to lift the cable, but to no avail. It was embedded in the sand! Cold chills crept up his body. The tide was beginning to wash across his feet. He was frightened. He knew he had to get out of there quickly. He waited for the water to cover his foot, thinking it would cool off and get a little smaller, but it didn't. The tide kept coming in. It was almost up to his knees.

There were some men fishing off shore. He called to them, but before he could make them understand, the tide had reached above his knees. He had been there for over an hour. The tide kept coming in. The men came to him. He told them his predicament. They tried to lift the cable but could not budge it. The tide kept creeping up.

One of the men waded to the shore, ran to the village and brought a blacksmith with a saw to cut the cable. The blacksmith had to work in the water. Something happened, and the saw snapped. There was just one more thing to do! The man made for the village again to bring the doctor. By the time he got back, the water was more than waist high. The village doctor tried to cut off the man's leg, but he couldn't work in the water. Those poor people had to stand by and see the French captain drown. He was enslaved by that cable.

* * *

DEVIL'S DAY

In the Far East there is a place where, once a year, they let the people do as they please and say what they please. The place is full of uproar, misrule and wickedness. They call it the "Devil's Day."

* * *

DEVOTION, 1

When Luther was about to start for Augsburg the princes tried to dissuade him from going. They said "At Augsburg are the powers of hell."

But Luther, in triumphant tones, replied, "At Augsburg Jesus reigns."

* * *

DEVOTION, 2

After Savanarola had adopted the religious life, we are told that his parents were terribly distressed. His message to them was: "If some temporal lord had girt me with a sword, and welcomed me among his followers, you would have regarded it as an honour to your house, and rejoiced. Yet now that the Lord Jesus Christ has girt me with His sword and dubbed me His knight, ye shed tears of mourning."

* * *

DEVOTION, 3

When William Lloyd Garrison, in his great anti-slavery crusade, addressed a great meeting in Washington, he exclaimed, "Where you stand I cannot tell, but I am in this fight to the end." Where do you stand?

* * *

DEVOTION, 4

Some of his friends once asked Coleridge for a proof of Christianity. Instead of entering into a discussion on the question, he simply replied: "Try it."

* * *

DIRECTION

As a prosperous New Yorker and his wife came to the small town where they had grown up, he said to her complacently, "Well, that's where we came from, dear."

She replied with an unexpected answer: "Yes, and I am just wondering where we got to."

* * *

DYING, 1

A man promised a pastor that he would not drink again. After the pledge had been taken the man appeared in late evening and said he must have a drink or he would die. The pastor told him to go home and die, and went on with his work. The next day the man appeared, smiling radiantly.

* * *

DYING, 2

Among the effects of James Russell Lowell were found these lines:

"Here lies a part of J. R. L.
The things that kept him from doing well."

* * *

ABILITY, 1

A physician gets nation wide reputation and honor, not by curing a case of measles or whooping cough, but by restoring a man whom all doctors despaired of or by performing an operation that was believed impossible.

* * *

ABILITY, 2

A lawyer obtains national fame not by the winning of a few petty cases in some small county court but by the skillful and successful management of some great case in chancery or by his wonderful speech on behalf of a criminal which saves the man's life after the country and bar has said he was doomed.

* * *

BACKSLIDING

Professor Summer said: "I never consciously gave up a religious belief. It was as if I had put my beliefs in a drawer, and when I came again to look for them the drawer was empty."

* * *

BLOOD CURE

(*I John* 1:7)

It was Charles G. Finney who told this story. He was holding a revival in Detroit. One night as he started to walk into the church, a man came up to him and asked, "Are you Dr. Finney?"

"Yes."

"I wonder if you will do me a favor. When you get through tonight, will you come home with me and talk to me about my soul?"

"Gladly. You wait for me." Finney walked inside, Some of the men stopped him.

"What did the man want, Brother Finney?"

"He wanted me to go home with him."

"Don't do it."

"I am sorry, but I promised and I shall go with him."

When the service was over, Finney started for the door.

The man was waiting, took his arm, and said, "Come with me."

They walked three or four blocks, turned into a side street, walked down an alley, and at the second house the man stopped.

"Stay here a minute, Brother Finney."

He reached into his pocket, pulled out a key, unlocked the door, turned to the preacher and said, "Come in." Mr. Finney walked into the room. There was a carpet on the floor, a fireplace, a desk, a swivel chair and two armchairs —nothing else. There was a thin partition around the room except for where the fireplace was. Finney turned around. The man had locked the door, had reached into his back pocket, had pulled out a revolver and was holding it in his hand.

"I don't intend to do you any harm," he said. "I just want to ask you some questions. Did you mean what you said in your sermon last night?"

"What did I say? I have forgotten."

"You said, 'The blood of Jesus Christ cleanses us from all sin.' "

Finney said, "Yes, God says so."

The man said, "Brother Finney, you see this revolver? It is mine. It has killed four people. Two of them were killed by me, two of them by my bartender in a brawl in my saloon. Is there hope for a man like me?"

Finney said, "God says, 'The blood of Jesus Christ his Son cleanseth us from all sin.' "

The man said, "Brother Finney, another question. In back of this partition is a saloon. I own it, everything in it. We sell every kind of liquor to anyone who comes along. Many, many times I have taken the last penny out of a man's pocket, letting his wife and children go hungry. Many times women have brought their babies here and pleaded with me not to sell any more booze to their husbands, but I have driven them out and kept right on with the whiskey selling. Is there hope for a man like me?"

Finney said, "God says, 'The blood of Jesus Christ his Son cleanseth us from all sin.' "

"Another question, Brother Finney. In back of this other partition is a gambling joint, and it is as crooked as sin, as crooked as Satan. There isn't a decent wheel in the whole place. It is all loaded and crooked. A man leaves the saloon with some money left in his pocket, and we take his money away from him in there. Men have gone out of that gambling place to commit suicide when their money and perhaps entrusted funds were all gone. Is there any hope for a man like me?"

Finney said, "God says, 'The blood of Jesus Christ his Son cleanseth us from all sin.' "

"One more question, and I'll let you go. When you walk out of this alley, you turn to the right toward the street, look across the street, and there you will see a two-story brownstone house. It is my home. I own it. My wife is there, and my eleven-year-old child, Margaret. Thirteen years ago I went to New York on business. I met a beautiful girl. I lied to her. I told her I was a stock broker. She married me. I brought her here. When she found out my business it broke her heart. I have made life a hell on earth for her. I have come home drunk, beaten her, abused her, locked her out, made her life more miserable than that of any brute beast. About a month ago I went home one night drunk, mean, miserable. My wife got in the way somehow, and I started beating her. My daughter threw herself between us. I slapped that girl across the face and knocked her against a red-hot stove. Her arm is burned from shoulder to wrist. It will never look like anything decent. Brother Finney, is there hope for a man like me?"

Finney got hold of that man's shoulders, shook him, and said, "O son, what a black story you have to tell! But God says, 'The blood of Jesus Christ his Son cleanseth us from all sin.'"

The man said, "Thank you. Thank you very much. Pray for me. I am coming to church tomorrow night."

Finney went about his business. The next morning, about seven o'clock, the saloon keeper started across the street out of his office. His necktie was awry. His face was dusty, sweaty, tear-stained. He was shaking, rocking as though he were drunk. But meanwhile he had taken the swivel chair, smashed the mirror, the fireplace, the desk and the other chairs. He had smashed the partition on each side. Every bottle and barrel and bar and mirror in that saloon was shattered and broken. The sawdust was swimming in a terrible mixture of beer, gin whiskey and wine. In the gambling establishment the tables were broken up and the dice and cards were smoldering in the fireplace. He staggered across the street, walked up the stairs of his home, and sat down heavily in the chair in his room. His wife called the little girl. "Maggie, run upstairs and tell Daddy breakfast is ready." The girl walked slowly up the stairs. Half afraid, she stood in the door and said, "Daddy, Mamma said breakfast was ready, for you to come down."

"Maggie darling, Daddy doesn't want any breakfast."

That little girl didn't walk; she flew down the stairs. "Mamma, Daddy said, 'Maggie darling,' and he didn't —"

"Maggie, you didn't understand. You go back upstairs and tell Daddy to come down." Maggie went back upstairs with the mother following her. The man looked up as he heard the child's step and said, "Maggie, come here."

Shyly, frightened, in a tremble, the little girl walked up to him. He lifted her, put her on his knee, pressed his face against her breast, and wept. The wife, standing in the door, didn't know what had happened. After awhile he noticed her and said, "Wife, come here." He sat her down on his other knee, threw his big man's arms around those two whom he loved, whom he had so fearfully abused, lowered his face between them, and sobbed until the room almost shook with the impact of his emotion.

After some minutes he controlled himself, looked up into the faces of his wife and girl, and said, "Wife, daughter, you needn't be afraid of me any more. God has brought you a new man, a new daddy, home today."

That same night the man, his wife and their child walked down the aisle of the church, gave their hearts to Christ and joined the church.

* * *

FAILURE

The late Dr. A. C. Dixon often told of an experience he had with his little boy. He was about to leave home and told the lad to take good care of his mother while he was gone. Later, when the doctor returned, Mrs. Dixon related the prayer the little fellow had said, "Dear Lord, please help and bless Daddy, and take good care of my sisters; but You do not need to mind about Mamma, for I can take care of her myself, for Daddy asked me to."

So long as we think we can take care of God's work without His help we are doomed to failure.

* * *

FAITH, 1

The late Dwight L. Moody was conducting a great religious campaign in Chicago during the World's Fair Exposition in 1893. He had brought great religious leaders from all over the world—and that was an expensive undertaking. On a certain day many bills and salaries had to be paid. Moody needed $3,000.00 to meet his financial obligations. Mr. Moody, with some other Christian workers, knelt down and prayed about the matter. The evangelist prayed in his unique way: "O Lord, I am sorely in need of money; I must have $3,000.00 today. I could raise it if I had time to go out after it, but, Lord, I'm booked to preach at the Great Northern Theatre at noon today and its half-past eleven now, and I must be there at twelve. Now Lord, in Thine own way, as Thou hast so often done before, please send me the needed money to carry on Thy work. Lord, I thank Thee that Thou hast heard me." And he arose, picked up his hat, and went down to the theatre to preach.

While he was on the stage waiting to preach, a lady came to one of the ushers and asked him to take her to Mr. Moody, for she had a message for him that must be delivered to him in person. The usher, naturally, refused, and said he would take the note to Mr. Moody. But the lady's persistence won out, and the usher took her to Mr. Moody to whom she handed an envelope. Mr. Moody, thinking it was a question someone wanted to ask him and not having time to attend to it at the moment, put the envelope in his pocket, and proceeded to preach.

When Mr. Moody, later, came to the dinner table with his fellow-workers, he remarked, "Oh, I had an envelope handed me today; I wonder what it is about?" He opened it, and to his surprise there was a check for $3000.00 signed by Mrs. Cyrus W. McCormick, wife of the harvesting machine manufacturer.

Mr. Moody went at once to see Mrs. McCormick. She told him that at about eleven thirty (the very hour that Mr. Moody and his workers had been in prayer) something told her that Mr. Moody would be needing money since he was conducting such an extensive campaign; so she sat down and wrote a check for $1000.00. Then a second thought came to her — that she should enlarge the amount of the check. So she tore up the $1000.00 check and made a new one for $2000.00. Again another thought pressed upon her, and led her to tear up that check also. She then made a new check for $3000.00, put it in an envelope, stamped it and rang for her servant to mail the letter. Then another thought came to her: *perhaps Mr. Moody needs this money today.* So she found out where Mr. Moody was preaching at that hour and sent her maid with the letter, giving her strict instructions to see that the letter was placed in Mr. Moody's own hands.

* * *

FAITH, 2

Faith is necessary for salvation:

A man is hanging by his hands, holding to a feeble vine on the side of a smooth perpendicular wall of a gigantic precipice, whose summit and boundaries are almost out of sight. Beneath him is a chasm, vast, deep, dark and wide. Pale with terror, there he hangs with no crevice in which to place his foot, swinging by his hands to a single, dry, withered vine growing out of a small fracture high above his head. He looks to the right and left, he sees nothing but a ledgeless cliff widening into tangled brushwood at its far extremes. He looks down with a sickening and reeling brain into the black rugged chasm over whose jaws he is swinging in horror. He looks above, and an unscalable precipice of rocks towers hundreds of feet above and forms the frowning crest of some mountain spur. There he swings, ever and anon a fibre of the creaking vine snaps, and cold chills course through his every vein.

He feels he cannot save himself. He looks around him and below him for help, but there is none. He looks above and beholds a light glittering and spangling down the rocks, and a strong angel shaving the dizzy cliff with broad wings of flashing alabaster, and coming to rest in perfect balance, every dazzling plume quivering in the subtle air, just beyond his reach over his head.

"Save me!" cried the frightened man.

"Do you believe I am able to do it?" replies the angel.

The man sees in a glance the strong wing and mighty arm, and answers, "I do."

"Do you believe I am willing to do it?" asks the angel.

The man gazes at the benign and loving face and answers, "I believe that thou are willing to do it."

"Then," says the angel, "*Let go.*" If the man believes in the ability and willingness of the angel to save him he will "let go" and depend upon the angel to catch him at the end of his own dependence, and in the act of his perfect faith.

* * *

FEARLESSNESS

(*Ps.* 23:4)

There is a wonderful little illustration about the small boy who came to a party and played until it grew dark. He knew he had to leave. He stood with his little face pressed against the glass of the door. His hostess came to him and asked, "What is the matter?"

"Well, it is time for me to go home."

But he was afraid. Between the house where he was playing and his home there was a cemetery. The little boy would have to walk through it all by himself, and he was frightened at the thought of the long, lonely, dark walk among the tombstones. The woman realized his fright and felt sorry for the lad.

"Son, don't be afraid," she said, "When you get ready to go home, tell me, and I will go, or my husband will go, or big brother will go."

The little fellow brightened up and went back to his games. An hour passed. He stood before the woman, cap in hand.

"Ma'm" he said, "thank you for the ice-cream, thank you for the cake, thank you for the present. I am going home."

"Darling, you know you'll have to walk in the dark through the cemetery. Something might happen to you."

The boy said, "I'll go; I'm not afraid."

She was unwilling to let him go. Anything might happen to an eight-year-old child, walking through the dark, ghostly graveyard. "No, wait, I'll send my husband with you."

The little boy said, "I'm not afraid because Mamma sent my big brother to take me home."

He was not afraid. I am not afraid either. I am not afraid of sickness, nor of old age, nor of poverty. I am not afraid. I am not afraid of any tombstone, not afraid of any graves, my own or that of anyone else, because my Big Brother has His hand on mine and there isn't anything that can hurt Him, not anything. He will take care of me. That is what I mean when I say if you are born again the Lord will watch over your present needs.

* * *

FOLLY

Out of the window of a little girl's room there could be seen a mountain beside the sea. She prayed one night, within her mother's hearing, that God would please cast that mountain into the sea. "Why do you offer a prayer like that?" asked her mother. "Why do you want that mountain to be cast into the sea?"

"Oh," said the little girl, "I'd just love to see the big splash it would make in the sea."

* * *

FOR CHRIST'S SAKE

II Corinthians 5:14, 15

Some years ago, in my wife's home town in Maine, a young man, who had just graduated from the Boston Technological Institute, was offered a job in a bank in Boston by one of his mother's old friends. He was to leave during the week. On Wednesday his mother came to his room as he was packing and said, "Son, they are showing a painting in the department store in town that I want you to go and see."

He said, "Mother, I am so busy packing; I have an engagement today for tea; and then there is a party tonight; and I am leaving tomorrow. I have no time for pictures."

She reached up, pulled him down, kissed him, and said, "Son, by this time tomorrow you will be so far away I won't be able to ask you any more favors. Please do this for me."

He said, "When you ask like that, I have to do it."

He went into the department store. The painting was on the fifth floor. They showed him the room. The door was closed. He knocked on the door again and again. Finally he pushed the door open, took a few steps in, and walked back out. There was somebody kneeling in prayer in that room. He knocked again and looked in. That somebody was still praying. Fifteen or twenty minutes had passed. He pushed the door open again, made a noise with his feet, cleared his throat, fumbled with the newspaper in his hand, but the man was still praying. He was about to touch the man on the shoulder and ask him about the painting, when lo and behold, he found it was the painting. The kneeling figure was the portrait. It was so beautifully displayed, so artistically lighted, that it looked for all the world like a living, breathing man in prayer.

No one came into that room. The boy took off his hat and held it in his hand. He began to cry and after a while walked backwards out of the room, closing the door. All that afternoon and night he thought about the picture. He did not enjoy himself at that party and he did not get much sleep.

The next morning at the breakfast table he spoke to his mother, "I don't have to be in Boston until Monday. I don't have to leave until Saturday. Mother, will you go with me and see that picture?"

They went to town and walked into the room. The mother stood on one side of the painting and the son on the other. The pathos, the concern, the anxiety of that kneeling form again moved the boy's heart. This time he bowed his head and sobbed like a broken-hearted child. The mother did not know what was taking place in her boy's heart, but she knew there was a storm there. After a while he looked up to say,

"Mother why is that man's form so sad, and His face so sorrowful, and His hands so pleading?"

"Son," she said, "this is Jesus praying in the Garden of Gethsemane. Son, He is thinking about the Cross on the morrow and is praying that God might give Him the grace to die like a man, not like a coward. Son, He is thinking of all those generations of men, women and children who are to come, who will need to know the story of that Cross, and is praying that God might raise up in every city, country, climate, nation, men, women, even children, who will give themselves to the telling of the story of the Cross."

The boy bowed his head and wept again. Then he looked up, clasped his hands and, looking into the face of the figure in that picture, said, "Blessed Master, if there is anything that You have left undone that I can do, count on me."

* * *

FREEDOM

Some years ago Dr. A. T. Schofield, a medical man of London and a devoted Christian, had a spirited dog, Jok by name. The dog was so spirited that the only way he could be controlled was by means of a leash. So it was the doctor's habit to take him for a daily walk, the master at one end of the leash and the dog at the other. No other procedure appeared practical. One day the master opened the door and offered the dog his freedom. How he bounded forth to enjoy his new-found freedom! Was he not at liberty at last? When he had gone a block or so, still within the range of his master's voice, the dog heard his name called, "Jok." As though pierced by an electric shock the dog stopped in his tracks, dropped his tail and meekly retraced his steps to his master's side.

* * *

FRUIT

The blessings of reproduction come to those who love the Lord and who wait on the Lord. Things in nature grow like their surroundings. Polar bears are white as snow; caterpillars are like the green leaves on which they feed.

* * *

GIVING

Dr. Alfred Adler, who was the originator of the phrase, "inferiority complex," attributed all human failure to inability to grasp the fact that "It is more blessed to give than to receive."

* * *

GOD'S LAW

Sophocles said: "The unwritten law of God that knows not change is,

They are not of today nor yesterday,
But live forever, nor can man assign
When first they sprang to being."

* * *

GRASS

Of all the things that come back to us from their long exile in the regions of winter, not the least pleasant, not the least welcome is the lowly grass. It is the last to leave he tribes of life take their departure. When the nes in with his soft-footed frosts, and his careen- asts, and when his onset grows deadlier day by day, one after another of the green things growing fail and flee, the grass holds its ground till all the rest have gone. Bravely it covers the retreat of its kindred; its green pennants wave in the rear of the flying foliage and the departing bloom. The brave beauties that held their heads so high in the soft days of spring and the proud days of midsummer vanish long before the grass surrenders; the forests, after all their songs of battle, and their boastful notes of victory over winds and snows, have already folded their splendid banners for many a day while the grass still keeps guard over the graves of the dead flowers. Grass is the last to depart and the first to return.

* * *

GRATITUDE

II Cor. 5:14, 15

I had been in this country about two years, maybe a little longer (the war was on in Europe) when the newspapers in Chicago came out with the awful statement that the young daughter of a local millionaire could not walk, that she was paralyzed. The girl was sent to the greatest surgeons, hospitals and sanitariums in America. It was of no use.

One section of the paper in Chicago came out picturing the girl in a wheelchair, saying that the chances were she never would walk. Just about that time there came into prominence that great Austrian physician, Dr. Lorenz. The girl's father paid him twenty thousand dollars as a fee and brought him to America. He took her to Vienna operated on her, brought her back in six months, and the girl could now walk with just a slight limp.

In those days, in Chicago, back of the stockyards, there used to be a section — poor, impossibly poor beyond description. We called it the Shanty Irish section. It was just dirt poor, poorer than poor. In the poorest home of that poor section, there lived a widow and her fourteen-year-old boy, Michael. He, too, had paralysis — got it in an accident. He had been confined to his bed. They were so poor they couldn't buy a wheel-chair. The mother had to carry him to the table, or outside for an airing. One day the mother came from her work and found Michael sitting up in bed, crying, a newspaper spread on his knees.

"What is the matter, Michael?" She looked at the paper. The war in Europe, strikes, divorce, automobile accidents — nothing unusual appeared on the page. "What are you crying about?"

He pointed down. She looked and there was an article describing the marvelous cure of the rich man's daughter.

"Son, that is something to praise the saints over."

"Mamma, wouldn't it be wonderful if that doctor would operate on me and make me walk?"

The heart of that poor mother rose in her throat. "They paid him twenty thousand dollars, and we don't have twenty thousand pennies," she said.

He looked up and said, "Mamma, can't a guy even wish?" She could stand no more. Running out the door, she leaned up against the wall of the house and wept. God gave her an idea. She went down town to Michigan Boulevard, walked into the Blackstone Hotel, and asked for the doctor's suite. She threw herself on her knees before that doctor. He could hardly speak English but between him and his secretary they learned what she wanted. He called her and asked her some questions.

He said, "Madam, do you have any money?"

She threw herself down again, and did everything but kiss his shoes, pleading and begging.

"Not for me," said Dr. Lorenz; "I don't want any money. It is to go to the hospital for the X-ray, the laboratory, for bandages, for the nurses. Not for me."

She kept on crying. He turned to his secretary and said something. The secretary got his hat and coat. Together with the woman, he went to examine Michael. He examined Michael, called an ambulance and took the boy to the West Side Free Hospital.

Dr. Lorenz stayed in the United States for eleven weeks, working on that boy, and Michael was restored to health. One day the boy was sitting in his wheel-chair when his mother came to visit him. They greeted each other.

After they had talked awhile, the boy said, "Mamma, go to the third window and look out."

"Why?"

"Never mind; you go and don't turn around."

"All right."

"Don't turn around."

In less time than it takes for me to tell you of it, she felt a touch on her sleeve. She looked up and found that Michael had walked across the room. Other visitors had to come running and lead the woman outside because from a law-abiding Catholic she had become a shouting Methodist! She hugged, and kissed, and petted that boy, pulled him to her. God had given her her boy almost from the dead. He could walk.

The days went on. One afternoon Dr. Lorenz came walking into the boy's room. "Son, I am leaving. I am going back to Vienna to my wife, my children, my work, my hospital, my people. You are going to be a good boy. You will be all right now, and the doctors will take care of you. In a few days you will go home."

Before he realized what the boy was doing, the doctor felt his hand being grasped in the lad's two hands and a passionate kiss being pressed on the back of it.

"You musn't do that," said the doctor, as embarrassed as any man would be.

The boy, tears coursing down his cheeks, said, "Doctor, as long as there is a tongue wagging in this head, there ain't nobody ever going to hear the last of what you have done for me."

* * *

GROWTH

Growth is an absolute necessity. How useful is the seed of cotton you plant until it grows out and up? How much would you give for it? Born in Christ we are mere babes, as newly planted fields. Whoever heard of expecting a wee mite of a baby to have full mental and physical powers? Whoever heard of expecting to harvest a field of corn or pick a field of cotton that was planted but yesterday? As the babe grows in years and strength, as the sun and the rain and the passing seasons develop the cotton and corn, even so must you and I grow and develop in the new life Christ Jesus has given us.

* * *

GUIDANCE

We are told that during the last World War a man was sent to lecture to the soldiers on the subject of astronomy — the position of the stars in the heavens and how by their position they could guide man and show him his position in time of danger and need. The soldiers thought it was foolish to sit there and listen to a lecture on the stars in the heavens. What they wanted to know, so it seemed to them at the moment, was how to get out of the mud in the trenches.

One night, a number of these same soldiers were sent out to reconnoiter. After crawling along the ground for some hours, they were discovered by the enemy, and were being fired on. They determined to return to their camp, but — where was the camp? Then, in their desperation, they remembered the lecture on the stars. They looked up to the heavens and saw, according to the position of the stars, that they were creeping toward the enemy instead of away from him. So they reversed their movements and after some time reached their own camp in safety.

* * *

HEAVEN'S GREATEST BID

Isaiah 52:3

Dr. Talmadge once made the following statement while addressing a certain gathering: "It seems to me as if all heaven were trying to bid in your soul. The first bid it makes is the tears of Christ at the tomb of Lazarus; but that is not a high enough price. The next bid heaven makes is the sweat of Gethsemane; but it is too cheap a price. The next bid heaven makes seems to be Christ's whipped back in Pilate's hall; but it is not a high enough price. Is it possible that heaven cannot buy you in?

"Heaven tries once more. It says, 'I bid this time for that man's soul the tortures of Christ's martyrdom, the blood on His temple, the blood in rills, the blood in pools, coagulated beneath the Cross; the blood that wet the tips of the soldiers' spears, the blood that splashes warm on the face of His enemies.'"

* * *

HOPELESS

One December day, Harriet Martineau wrote her friend, saying: "For England the summer has gone, and for me the everlasting winter has set in."

* * *

JOY

A man traveling through the South called a Negro from the station platform to the train window and asked: "Uncle, is there anybody in this town enjoying religion?"

The old Negro replied, "Them's that's got it, is."

* * *

INFIDEL

It is told of a certain man in Scotland, who was in the habit of making loud pretensions of being an infidel, that his only son went over with the first contingent to France, to fight in Flanders Field in the first World War. It was announced that prayers would be offered in all the churches, on a certain Sunday, for the brave boys over in France. All who believed in prayer were invited to come.

Among those present was this professing infidel, the man who had always made a mock of prayer. A friend, noticing him in the church, was greatly surprised and said, "Well, my friend, I am surprised to see you here, for you have so often asserted that you did not believe in God or prayer."

"Oh, well," replied the infidel, "circumstances alter cases. You know I have a boy over there, and I fear the worst for him, and so I know of no one else to talk to about him but the One who is above; so I came to ask your God to take care of my boy."

* * *

INFIDEL — VOLTAIRE

Voltaire once stood watching a funeral procession. As a hugh crucifix, carried by four men, passed by, Voltaire was seen to raise his hat and hold it aloft in the air until the crucifix had passed. A friend of his, noticing this, said, "Well, are you at last a believer in God?"

"No," replied the atheist. "We salute, but we do not speak."

* * *

INTERCESSION

I John 5:14-16

Who that has ever heard or read the story of John and Mary Welch, the daughter and son-in-law of John Knox, can forget its moving details? You will recall that John was a sickly, anemic, consumptive, non-conformist preacher in the time of James of Scotland, when the Catholic Church ruled the land. John had been imprisoned for preaching the Gospel. The filth, the darkness, the dampness of his underground cell robbed him of what little health he had, so that he almost died. Time and again Mary appealed to the king for his release, only to be refused. One day, in her desperation, she threw herself on her knees in front of the king as he was riding through the palace park. The king reined in his horse and asked her what she wanted. Once more she told him the pathetic plight of her husband and begged for his discharge from prison.

After considering a moment, the king made her an offer. "Woman," he said, "if you will promise that your husband will never preach again, I will open the doors of his cell at once."

Mary rose to her feet. Lifting her apron, she threw back her head and looked fully and fearlessly into James' face. "Your Majesty," she cried, "I would rather have the head of my husband in this apron than to make any such promise."

Moved by the intensity of the woman, the king released John into her custody. She took him back to their home in the Scottish highlands and carefully, gently, lovingly nursed him back to health. He began to preach again, keeping one jump ahead of the police and the dragoons. One night the two found themselves hidden in a small highland cottage. It was a freezingly cold night. They had gone to bed early. In the middle of the night, Mary awoke to find her husband had apparently disappeared. She heard a sound on the floor and looked down. There was John stretched out on that frozen earth floor, wrapped in a spread, weeping and groaning in prayer. She urged him to return to bed lest he take cold. He said something to her which she took as a sign of assent and fell asleep once more. The morning sun woke her. John was still on the floor, deep in agonizing prayer. She bent and touched his shoulder, urging him to get under the covers. He lifted his twisted, tear-stained face to her and said, "O woman, let me alone. I have three thousand souls on my heart this night, and I know not how it is with many of them."

That is compassion — the burning, yearning, driving, longing, constraining desire for the souls of men.

* * *

INVITATION

Rev. 22:17

A young girl living in a Western town quarreled with her mother. She left home in a rage and went to New York City. Tired of working, or perhaps unable to find work, she descended into deep sin. She drank. She caroused. Her life was steeped in iniquity. The mother continued to weep and pray over her prodigal daughter. She tried every means to locate the young woman and bring her home. Finally, at the suggestion of her pastor, she had a number of photographs made of herself and scattered them from one end of the country to the other. She sent them to hotels, to mission halls and to Y.W.C.A.'s, with the hope and prayer that the girl would see one of them and be moved to return. Across the front of every picture she wrote two words: "Come home." She signed the message "Mother."

One night the girl was returning home half drunk from a wild orgy. As she staggered along she passed the lighted window of a mission. Glancing at it, she saw a photograph across the page of an open Bible. The girl walked past but something pulled her back. The face on the picture was strangely familiar. It was late and the mission was locked. The next day she came back and the mission director told her that it was her mother. He had recognized the girl from the description on the back of the photograph. The pathetic expression on the mother's face broke the heart of the daughter, and in the mission she wept out her repentance and remorse. The superintendent somehow raised enough money to pay the girl's fare to her home. Buying her ticket, he put her on the homeward-bound train.

Arriving at her destination, the girl stepped off the train and walked down the street to her home. Her heart was heavy. Her soul was torn. She did not know what to expect. Hesitantly she knocked on the door. The mother threw open the door, recognized the daughter and with passionate tears and kisses gave the girl her full love and entire forgiveness. There was no criticism, no abuse. The aching, longing, yearning heart of the mother was filled with grace and compassion for the daughter, and the pain and bitterness of the terrible months spent in sin were forgotten.

Beloved, this story portrays the love of God. He wants us home. If you accept His invitation, He will not talk about your sins, but about your salvation. He will not discover your shortcomings, but speak of your sanctification. There will be no abuse: there will be no remonstrance. The patient heart of God will press you to itself. He will kiss away the stains of your soul. He will strip you of the rags of evil and clothe you in the robes of righteousness. He will put the ring of adoption upon your finger and the shoes of satisfaction on your feet. He will call the angels together to rejoice over a sinner who has come home.

* * *

LIVING IN THE SPIRIT

"Ye are not in the flesh but in the spirit if so be that the spirit of God dwell in you" — the sponge in the water — the water in the sponge. The poker in the fire — the fire in the poker. If the Christian is in Christ — Christ is in the Christian. If the believer is in the Spirit — the Spirit is in the believer.

* * *

MIND

Do you remember Clifford Beers' story *A Mind That Found Itself?* Clifford was a sensitive lad who had an older brother with epilepsy. The younger boy lived in dread terror that he too might become an epileptic. This terror was so dreadful to him that he did not dare to speak about it to anyone, but, instead, brooded upon it within his imagination in morbid and melancholy solitude until it began to take on the shape and form of the actual. I can just see him sitting there in the classrooms of Yale University with this freezing horror at his heart. "I was an epileptic — doomed to what I then considered a living death," he writes, "I thought epilepsy, I dreamed epilepsy, until thousands of times during the six years that this disquieting idea persisted, my overwrought imagination seemed to drag me to the very verge of an attack."

The consequence was three years in an insane asylum. Yet Clifford Beers has come back. How close a call it was! He was in the grip of that deep tendency in human nature to become the life that you imagine yourself to be.

* * *

NEED

A psychiatrist in Hollywood, who is paid handsomely by his disrupted filmdom patients, said, "Most of my patients do not need me; they need a mourner's bench; they need God."

* * *

OBEDIENCE, 1

A man stood one day at the corner of a street in an eastern city waiting for the street car. As a car approached the man waved to the motorman to stop, but the car sped on its journey without slowing down. The man thought perhaps the car had been delayed on its way and was trying to make up for lost time. So he waited for another car. In a few moments one appeared in the distance. The man waved his hand again, and again the car sped on without stopping. He then began to complain inwardly about the carelessness of motormen and the service. He waited for another car. While he was waiting a man came up to him and said, "My friend, I noticed you waved to the motorman to stop the car. He cannot do it here; you will have to go to the next block, the cars stop there."

The man could have been standing at that street corner yet and no cars would have stopped for him. It was necessary for him to obey the law of the streetcar company if he would board one of the cars.

* * *

OBEDIENCE, 2

Genesis 31:16

A Negro preacher once said, "Breaven, whateber de good God tell me to do in dis blessed Book, dat I'm gwine to do. If I see in it dat I must jump troo a stone wall, I'm gwine to jump at it. Going troo it belongs to God; jumpin' at it 'longs to me."

* * *

OBEDIENCE, 3

The following story about a shepherd and his sheep may help us to a better understanding of God's dealings with His people.

A lady was spending the summer in Switzerland. One day she started out for a stroll. Presently, as she climbed the mountainside, she came to a shepherd's fold. She walked to the door and looked in. There sat the shepherd. Around him lay his flock. Near at hand, on a pile of straw, lay a single sheep. It seemed to be suffering. Scanning it closely, the lady saw that its leg was broken. At once her sympathy went out to the suffering sheep. She looked up inquiringly to the shepherd.

"How did it happen?" she asked.

To her amazement the shepherd answered: "Madam, I broke that sheep's leg."

A look of pain swept over the visitor's face. Seeing it, the shepherd went on: "Madam, of all the sheep in my flock this one was the most wayward. It would not obey my voice. It would not follow in the pathway in which I was leading the flock. It wandered on the verge of many a perilous cliff and dizzy abyss. And not only was it disobedient itself, but it was ever leading the other sheep astray. I had before had experience with sheep of this kind. So I broke its leg. The first day I went to it with food, it tried to bite me. I let it lie alone for a couple of days. Then I went back to it. That time, it not only took the food, but licked my hand, and showed every sign of submission and even affection.

"And, now, let me tell you something. When this sheep is well, as it soon will be, it will be the model sheep of my flock. No sheep will hear my voice so quickly. None will follow so closely at my side. Instead of leading its mates astray, it will now be an example and a guide for the wayward ones, leading them, with itself, in the path of obedience to my call. In short, a complete transformation will have come into the life of this wayward sheep. It has learned obedience through its sufferings."

* * *

OVERCOMING POWER

I Peter 1:3-5

It was Dr. Venting of the Southwestern Baptist Theological Seminary who told our class this story. Years ago he was pastor of the great, tremendously rich Euclid Avenue Baptist Church of Cleveland, Ohio. The organist of that church was a young, marvelously skilled musician named Roland. He was married, and had a beautiful wife and two precious children. He was not a Christian. His besetting, killing sin was drink. One Sunday night there was a baptismal service in the church. The crowd had gone when Dr. Venting stepped out of his dressing room through his study, through the auditorium to the rotunda of the church. Roland was just starting down the stairs.

Dr. Venting stopped him. They talked for a while about small things. Then the pastor began to plead with him for Christ. The night was beautiful. The Spirit of God seemed to be reaching down from the balmy skies. Roland was touched, moved, melted. The two men knelt in the shadow of a great column. Dr. Venting raised his voice in passionate prayer to God. When he was through, Roland gloriously accepted and confessed Christ as his personal Saviour.

The next morning Dr. Venting was walking to town to the ministerial conference when he noticed a familiar figure ahead of him. It was Roland. The preacher watched him. This took place before prohibition days, and there were numerous saloons, one to almost every block. The young organist walked up to the first saloon, stopped, started to go in, clenched his hands, shook them, turned around and walked on. He did that at least a half-dozen times before he came to the building where his studio was located. Dr. Venting kept on following him, entered the building just a few steps behind him, took the next elevator up and stepped into Roland's office.

"Good morning, Dr. Venting."

"Good morning, Roland. How do you feel this morning?"

"Oh, Dr. Venting, I am the happiest man in all the world. I did not know there could be such joy!"

"Roland, I wasn't spying on you, but tell me, what were you doing in front of those saloons when you stopped, started in, then turned away and walked on?"

The young musician colored like a schoolgirl. Great tears came to his eyes.

"Dr. Venting, Jesus and I were having a good time."

"What do you mean, Roland, 'Jesus and I were having a good time'?"

"Well, brother pastor, you know my sin, don't you?

That is what kept me from coming to Christ a long time ago. I did not want to be a hypocrite. I was worried about myself. This morning I knew I had to fight it out or it would whip me. I stopped in front of those saloons. The smell of gin, of wine, of beer — warm, tempting, tantalizing — assailed me. I could not keep from walking in. My strength was too small. It was then that I asked Jesus to give a guy a hand. Dr. Venting, He did. He kept the devil from me. He gave me grace to turn away, to go on."

Together in that modern office building the two men once more fell on their knees to lift up their grateful hearts and voices to God, to thank Him that Jesus is able to save from the power of sin.

* * *

PLEASING GOD

There was a certain gatekeeper at the Union Station in St. Louis. One bitterly cold night, as he required a showing of tickets, there was much grumbling and complaining over the inconvenience of removing gloves and unbuttoning coats. At length a passenger remarked, "You don't seem to be very popular around here tonight."

Pointing to the executive offices above, the gatekeeper replied, "There's one man up there whom I seek to please. Nothing else matters."

* * *

PRAYER, 1

It was Abraham Lincoln who said, "I have been driven many times to my knees by the overwhelming conviction that I had nowhere else to go. My own wisdom, and that of everyone around me, seemed insufficient for the day."

* * *

PRAYER, 2

Many a dying soldier boy has used his last breath on the field of battle to call on God. "Do you ever pray?" asked the chaplain of the dying soldier.

"Well, I prayed last night before we went over the top to take this fortified position of the enemy. I guess every fellow prays before a battle."

* * *

PRAYER, 3

A sceptical scientist, who had always provided amply for his son, allowing him to use all his pictures and books and instruments and library for the entertainment of his friends, was one day talking about religion with his son, who had become a Christian. They were talking about prayer. The father said he saw no reason whatever why he should ask God for what was already furnished in nature and which would come in the natural order of things.

To this the son replied, "Father, I remember that when once I made free use of your pictures and books to entertain my friends, you said to me, 'All I have belongs to you, my son, and I have provided it on purpose for you; still I think it would be respectful always to ask your father before taking anything.' "

The father was silent, and afterwards admitted not having been able to answer his son's sensible argument.

* * *

PRAYER, 4

It is told of Hudson Taylor that at one time his prayers were the direct means of delivering the ship that was conveying him to his distant field. After the ship had been long on its way, hindered by calms and contrary winds, an island was sighted. It was recognized as the abode of fierce cannibals, who knew no pity. Just at the time the wind died away and the vessel lay helpless on the glassy sea, slowly but surely drifting onto the fatal shore. With grim delight the island savages saw the plight of the ship and in sight of her crew made preparations for the coming feast of human flesh.

The captain sought his missionary passenger. "You believe that God hears prayer. Call on Him. Unless your praying is the real thing we are doomed."

"I will pray," quietly responded Mr. Taylor, "on condition that you set your sails to catch the breeze that God will send."

The captain, who was not a believer, refused to make a spectacle of himself by unfurling the sails in a dead calm. Mr. Taylor was equally firm in refusing to pray until the ship was put in readiness to avail itself to the answer. Nearer and nearer the shore they drifted, until in fear the captain unfurled the sails to receive the wind of which as yet they could see no sign.

Mr. Taylor retired to his cabin and laid the case before the Lord. He quoted the promises and asked that since He had brought him so far on his way, he might be permitted to carry on his work in the dark places of the earth. He, like Paul, besought the Lord to give him the lives of those on board. While he was still praying, there came a knock at the door. "Are you still praying for wind?" asked the voice of the captain.

"Yes," was the response.

"Well," said the captain, "you had better quit praying for we have more wind now than we can manage."

* * *

PRAYER, 5

Dr. William Evans has said, "Some people feel that it is too much to expect the Lord to keep track of all the people who want to pray."

Notice how absurd that is. The Chicago telephone company has over three hundred thousand subscribers. If all the people on the earth this very day should begin to pray, the problem would be only approximately five thousand times greater than that of Chicago telephone system: Is it hard to believe that the Lord who made the men who developed the Chicago telephone system can handle a proposition five thousand times greater than these men are handling successfully?

"Science tells us that if we put a common pin under a microscope we will discover as much activity going on there as among the stars. Here are electrons so numerous that the human race in a million years could not count them, and yet not one electron touches another. In comparison with their size they are as far apart as the planets of a solar system. Endlessly they revolve around each other, and not one ever slips by an infinitesimal degree from the control of law. It is not strong reason but weak imagination that leads us to be terrorized by the size of the universe and the thought that God does not or cannot care for us individually.

"I have heard some people say, 'I do not feel worthy to pray; I do not feel good enough to pray.' Do not forget that after the telephone company has installed a telephone they do not ask you whether you are good or not when you attempt to use the telephone."

* * *

REDEMPTION

Gal. 3:13

The Prison Walls Fall

It was a cold February morning before dawn during the second World War. Inside a guarded Air Force operations room were gathered several air-crews for briefing. There was an atmosphere of great tenseness as Group-Captain Pickard addressed his men.

"The objective," he said "is Amiens Prison, where over a hundred French patriots are waiting execution for assisting and concealing Allied airmen who have been brought down over France. The plan is to smash the prison and liberate these patriots.

"The huge walls are twenty feet high, and three feet thick, and these must be breached in at least two different places. The main building must be attacked at each end to release the doomed men.

"The time factor is most vital to secure the co-operation of those who will be waiting outside the prison."

The Group Captain finished with these words, "Boys you have to break that prison wide open."

An hour before noon the bomber squadrons left to link up with their fighter escort at the appointed rendezvous. The first six planes swept in to the north of Amiens and made straight for their objective. Their work was to breach the prison wall, while the second wing was left to divide and open up both ends of the jail and destroy the guards quarters. So low did the first machines fly that they were scarcely ten feet above the ground at times. A great gaping hole was torn in the wall, then another. Then the wing of the building was smashed. Over the snow-covered courtyard the prisoners dashed toward the holes. Several of the patriots fell, but the majority escaped.

Group-Captain Pickard had been directing the whole operation overhead. Just then one of the Mosquito bombers was shot down by flak, and the leader went to see what had happened to his men. While thus detached from fighter cover he was pounced upon by two F. W. 190's. Two of the Mosquitoes, one of them carrying the leader and his navigator, were shot down by enemy fighters. Also two of the fighter escort were shot down. That was the cost of this important mission.

The sacrifice was indeed great, for these men are among the finest of a nation's manhood; but it was not in vain. A high percentage of the patriots made good their escape and will yet be heard of for the part they are playing in the liberation of their country.

The bodies of the Group-Captain and his companions were recovered by friendly villagers, who were compelled to hand them over to the enemy. But that did not prevent the people from turning out enmasse to the cemetery near the prison and showing in a marked way their intense gratitude for the wonderful deliverance which had been wrought on their behalf.

* * *

REWARDS

At the close of the Crimean War, in 1855, England appointed a day in which to welcome her brave soldiers returning from the disastrous battles. Queen Victoria had Crimean medals struck off. Galleries were constructed for the two houses of Parliament and the royal family. The throng of thousands sang forth "God Save the Queen." Her Majesty came in, with her secretary, to bestow upon the soldiers their well-deserved rewards. What a sight it was! A colonel who had lost both his feet in the battle of Inkerman, wheeled in on a chair; a man whose arms were missing; others, variously maimed and halt.

Of them all, one stands out in remembrance. He was also an Inkerman hero. A cannon ball took off one of his legs, but he recovered his stand, took hold of a tree and continued to fight till another ball took his other leg. He was carried from the field, supposedly to die. But he recovered sufficiently to return home.

The Queen, knowing his story, saw him brought in, carried by four other men, his face as white as the stretcher's sheet on which he lay. Brushing aside her secretary she took the medal and with her own hands pinned it upon his breast. As his sovereign's tears of gratitude fell upon his face, what emotions filled that fellow's breast!

A great day for that soldier! Yes, indeed. But it dims before the brightness of that day awaiting us, if so be we have lived for Him.

* * *

SACRIFICE, 1

J. Wilbur Chapman records this incident: "When Booth was in this country, he told of a man leaving Australia who had been working in the gold fields, and had acquired a fortune. The ship he was on sprung a leak. The lifeboats were lost, and the people were without hope. This strong man thought he could fight through the waves to the island, and he was about to spring into the water, when a little bit of a girl, whose mother had been lost in the storm, asked of him, 'Sir, can you save me?'

"He looked at his belt, his belt of gold, and then at the child, and then at the belt, and then at the child again. And then he threw the belt of gold away, took her on his back, and threw himself into the sea. He struggled through; with life almost gone he reached the land. The next day, consciousness returned to him. The little girl put her arms around his neck, and her lips to his cheek, and said, 'I am so glad you saved me.' That was worth more than all the gold in Australia."

* * *

SACRIFICE, 2

A soldier returned from the World war minus one arm and both legs. One man said, "It is such a pity that you should have lost your limbs in the war."

"I did not lose them I gave them for my country."

"I gave, I gave my life for thee
What hast thou given for me?"

* * *

SACRIFICIAL LOVE

I John 4:9-10

A Russian nobleman, his wife, his two children and a servant were riding a sleigh pulled by four horses. A pack of ravenous wolves pursued them. The nearest town was miles away. The driver loosed one of the horses. This delayed the murderous beasts as they tore the horse to pieces, but only for a brief respite. A second horse was loosed to divert the ravenous brutes, but in a short time the wolves came on again. No other horse could be spared. The lights of the town appeared, but the wolves were gaining. The servant, turning to his master, released the reins into his hands. With a shouted farewell he jumped from the speeding sled and, drawing his axe from his belt, stood facing the oncoming horde. The fight was long. The snow became crimson with spurting blood, but the master, the mistress and the children were saved. The peasant had paid the last full measure of devotion. But he owed it. It was a matter of loyalty and allegiance. He was bound to his lord by a thousand bands of obedience and favors. It was not so with Jesus. He was not our servant, although He made Himself so. He owed us no debt of gratitude.

* * *

SATAN

As a master is bad, so his work is much worse and his wages worst of all. If Satan binds us, it is no matter to him whether it be by a cable or a hair. Christians should live in the world but not be filled with it. A ship lives in the water; but it goes to the bottom if the water gets into the ship.

* * *

SECURITY

One of the richest men of a Middle Western city wondered what he could give his daughter as a heritage. He began with financial securities, and went on down the list, but rejected all material legacies as too insecure. He finally fastened on Christianity as the only secure inheritance he could give his child — an interesting conclusion, for he himself was not born again.

* * *

SELF, 1

In the play *Peer Gynt,* the hero committed to the role that he would be "himself," visits a lunatic asylum. There, he assumes, people are "outside themselves."

The doctor corrects him: "It's here that men are most themselves — themselves and nothing but themselves — sailing with outspread sails of self. Each shuts himself in a cask of self, the cask stopped with a bung of self and seasoned in a well of self. None has a tear for other's woes or cares what any of the others think."

* * *

SELF, 2

The lie detector has shown that only three percent of employees in department stores are honest in character and that only five percent of tellers in banks would prove to be honest if there were no other measures for checking fraud.

* * *

SELF CONTROL

No man is free who cannot command himself.

—Conqueror Alexander, who died drunk.

* * *

SERVICE

Rom. 12:1-2

I had a friend, a lawyer, an international lawyer, a great man, tremendously wealthy, a good man. He came from Virginia. When he was twenty-four years old he married a beautiful girl. They were both good Christians, both saved. There was no doubt about it in anyone's mind. They lived right, did not gamble, did not drink, went to church, taught Sunday school classes. He got a job with a firm in New York, and they moved, changing their church membership to a church there.

They were childless. They had plenty of time, plenty of money. His business grew by leaps and bounds. It took him all over America. He loved to be near his wife, so he took her along. They stopped going to church, stopped praying, stopped teaching Sunday school classes. They gave more money than ever. They were clean morally. The man did not even smoke. He never tasted a drink. They never went to a dance. There was nothing the matter with their lives morally. It was just business. They were just out of the service of the Lord. On Sunday they would be in a strange town, business conferences and plans must be made, and so on.

One Christmas-time the man could not go home with his wife because of business, so she went alone for the holidays to visit their people. They lived in the same town. On the day after New Year's Day, she started back home. The train on which she was riding was wrecked. Her back was broken. Doctors, nurses, ambulances came. She was stretched out on the ground beside the track. A doctor came over. When he touched her she screamed in her pain. He tried to move her a bit, but she cried aloud and almost fainted. The conductor came up. The doctor said something to him. The conductor said, "Yes, tell her, she can stand it."

The doctor leaned over. "Lady," he said, "I am sorry but your back is broken. You are going to die. I can't even move you. There is nothing I can do."

She said, "My husband is very wealthy. You can spend all the money you want to, do anything you want to. If there is a chance, help me."

The doctor replied, "We would do it without money, but there is no chance. I will help you, make it easier on you, but I cannot move you."

There was nothing to do. The doctor went on to the others. Finally he came back. The lady had thrown her arm over her face, and was weeping, whispering something. He touched her, and asked her what she was saying.

She took her arm down, and said, "If I had only known, if I had only known, if I had only known."

He said, "What do you mean?"

"Oh, Doctor, if I had only known I was going to die so soon I would have given all of my time to the Lord."

* * *

SUITABLE FOOD

Plant some cotton in the clay and gravel roads that stretch all over Oklahoma and Texas. It will not grow or it will grow poorly. It needs rich loamy soil to produce the growth.

Plant the same cotton where the sun will never shine on it. It will not grow or grow poorly.

Plant this same cotton in the Great American Desert. It will perish for want of rain.

So is the Christian life in a soul. The seed needs good soil, sunshine and rain.

* * *

TESTIMONY, 1

Some people are like the man who had taken twenty bottles of Peruna. When Dr. Hartman asked him for a statement he said "Dear Dr. Hartman, I have taken twenty bottles of Peruna and can truthfully say that I have no worms, but I've got snakes."

* * *

TESTIMONY, 2

The Irishman kept yelling, "Hurrah for Ireland!" The Englishman got tired of it and said, "Hurrah for Hell."

Irishman: "That's right, every mon for his own country."

* * *

THROUGH TICKET

John 11:25

Some months ago I attended the great Southern Baptist Convention in Baltimore, Maryland. One early morning the Southwestern Baptist Theological Seminary group had its breakfast in one of the hotels. Dr. Scarborough, the president of the seminary, addressed the gathered group at the end of the breakfast. He reminded us of the blessings of God upon our alma mater. He told us how it was entwined in the very fibre of his heart, blazoned on the burning anxiety of his soul. He told us of some of his sacrifices, of his hopes, of his aspirations for the school. Standing before us, with tears streaming down his cheeks, he bade us recall his own age, his own fatigue and how soon he would have to drop the great load. He said:

"I am almost seventy. I believe I have done my part. By day and by night, at home and abroad, I have prayed, I have toiled, I have given of my heart's blood to the school. Perhaps very soon I shall have to lay my burden down. I shall have to go on up to be with Jesus. Before I go, I should like to know that the seminary is secure. I know reasonably well that I must go very soon."

He paused, bowed his head in silent meditation and prayer. When he looked up at us, great tears were chasing each other down his cheeks. "I do not want you to misunderstand, brethren and sisters," he said. "I am not talking about my death, primarily. I am not much concerned about it. I am not afraid to die. I have a through ticket." Again he grew silent, as with lowered head he stood before us. Once more he raised his eyes, and said, "I am not afraid to die, I have got a through ticket."

Each word dropped like fire into our souls. We thought of Calvary. We thought of Christ's torn body. We thought of His indescribable agony. We thanked God that we, too, had a "through ticket," written and signed in the Blood of the Lamb.

* * *

TRAVAIL

Isa. 66:8

In the South some years ago, one of our really great evangelists held a revival. The Lord's blessings were upon it. The crowds came. Scores were saved and added to the church. One evening, a young-appearing mother came to speak to the preacher.

"Sir," she said, "I should like to ask you a very vital question. I have three children—a girl six years old, a boy of twelve and another boy of fifteen. The little girl is perhaps too young to understand, but the boys are old enough to be saved. I've tried to talk to them about Christ and their souls, but they will not listen to me. They come to church all right, but they seem to be absolutely untouched. Tell me, what can I do with them?"

The evangelist studied the woman a moment. "Madam," he said, "may I ask you some questions? I presume you are a Christian. Is your husband?"

"Yes, sir, and one of the choicest souls I know. He is a deacon and teaches a Sunday school class."

"Do you have a family altar in your home? Do you have grace over meat?"

"Indeed we do, sir. We have family worship twice each day and grace at every meal."

"Do you go to church services consistently and take your children with you?"

"Brother preacher, I guess that perhaps our entire family are the most consistent attendants of the church services of anybody in the community. Our children always go when we go."

Again the evangelist studied the woman. "Sister," he said, "will you listen to a plain word without being offended?"

"Yes, sir, you can tell me anything you wish, and I shall

not feel hurt. Give me your very best advice, no matter what it may be."

"Madam, your children are not being saved because your eyes are dry." The preacher turned away, and the mother went home.

She wept and prayed all night long. The next morning she gave her husband his breakfast and waited for the children to get up. When they were all about the breakfast table, the mother turned to her older boy. "Johnnie, I've been praying as hard as I could that you might give your soul to Christ. Johnnie, will you take Christ as your Saviour?"

The younger boy, named Edwin, hastily stood up, pushed back his chair, dropped his napkin on the table, and ran out of the room. The mother paid no attention to him, but kept on pleading with the first son. The Lord had mellowed the boy's heart. After some minutes, the mother and son knelt by the side of the dining-room table, and the mother had the infinite joy of praying her son into the kingdom of God. Right then and there he accepted Christ.

Late that afternoon, while the mother was in the kitchen working over the evening meal, Edwin came in to throw himself on his mother's neck. "Mother," he cried, "I'm saved! I've been saved! I've accepted Christ as my Saviour! I am going forward tonight! Is Johnnie? Is Johnnie?"

"Yes, darling, Johnnie has given his heart to Jesus; but tell me, where have you been? What has happened to you?"

"Mamma, last night I could not sleep. I got up out of bed, started downstairs to go to the icebox to get something to eat, and some milk. I passed your door. I thought I heard you crying. I tiptoed in. You were stretched out on the floor praying, asking God to save Johnnie and me. I didn't go into the kitchen. I went back upstairs and cried myself to sleep. This morning when you started talking to Johnnie, I just could not stand any more. I ran out to the cotton patch and I've been there praying ever since. I have trusted Christ. I know Jesus has saved me."

That night that mother had the infinite joy of leading her two precious sons to the altar of God, to Christ and into the church. Beloved, I have been in all sorts of revivals, in churches, in brush arbors, in tents, in tabernacles, in school auditoriums, in theaters, in cotton sheds. I have seen landslides for Christ. I have had my heart broken many times over the paucity of results. After these few years of humble yet many experiences in preaching, I can sincerely, spiritually say I have never seen a revival of any size, of any great proportions, that was not paid for by the tears and the agony of some of God's people. We shall never win these great victories some of our hearts are longing for, dry-eyed. Gethsemane and Calvary must always precede Pentecost. We need travailing Christians.

* * *

WELCOME

A minister was riding in a train. The only occupant of the coach except himself was a young man who seemed exceedingly ill at ease. The young man would sit in one seat, get up and go to another, take up a book and drop it again. The minister went over and sat down beside him, asking what was wrong.

At first the boy would not answer, but at last the dam broke, and he burst forth with this story: "I've run away from home, and I've been away for a long time. I wanted to go back, and wrote my father asking if he would take me back. I told him that I would not wait for a reply, but would start for home, and that if he wants me back, to hang a white rag on the crabapple tree near the railroad tracks, so that I can see it when the train goes by. If the white rag is not there, I shall understand and go on by. We are getting near and I am afraid to look —afraid the white rag won't be there."

The minister told the lad he needn't look—that he would look for him. The boy sat with his eyes closed, the hand of the minister resting on his knee. As they drew near to where the tree was, the hand of the minister closed tight on the boy's knee, as he said, "My boy there is a white rag on every limb of that tree!"

* * *

WITNESSING

Acts 1:8

I have a dear preacher friend, Oby Nelson, a pastor in Royse City, Texas. We have been praying partners for many years. He told his story in a Baptist association meeting in Texas. When he was much younger, say, twenty years ago, Brother Nelson and another young preacher, John Skaggs, held a brush arbor meeting in one of the school communities on the Red River near Gainesville, Texas. People came. The Lord was with them. Souls were converted. One day, after the morning service, a young man told Brother Nelson that Bud Walker was coming to the mourner's bench that night for salvation. Now Bud was the deaf and dumb (from birth) son of a deacon of that community. Bud had not missed a service of the revival, but of course he had not heard a syllable of the proceedings. The two preachers, Nelson and Skaggs, walked over to where Bud was standing by a buggy and began talking to him.

"Bud do you know what it means to be a Christian? Are you ready to accept Christ as your Saviour?"

Bud opened his mouth, smiled widely, and made that awful, heart-rending sound that a deaf and dumb person makes when he tries to speak. The two preachers could clearly see that the boy neither understood them nor could he make himself understood. Not willing to give up too easily, the two preachers seated him in their buggy and drove over to his father's place. The old man was in the yard of his home working on some harness when they rode up.

"Mr. Walker, Bud wants to give his heart to Christ, and we want to be sure he knows what he is doing. Will you try to explain to him the meaning of being saved?"

The farmer looked out across his fields. His eyes filmed over with unshed tears. "Brother Nelson, and you, Brother Skaggs," he said, "I am fifty-three years old. Bud is twenty-four. I have been a Christian since I was nine, and a deacon for over thirty years. I can make that boy understand almost anything about the work of the farm, but I have never been able to explain Christ to him, and God knows I've tried. Perhaps his mother can. She is in the kitchen."

They walked into the kitchen. "Mother, Bud wants to be saved," said the old farmer. "We do not want to stand in his way, but we want to be sure he understands what he is doing. Can you ask him some questions about his soul and his sins, and about the Saviour?"

The mother covered her face with her apron and sobbed. After some minutes, her face streaked with tears, she turned to the preachers. "Brethren," she said, "I am forty-eight years old. I have been a Christian since I was eleven and a church-member all this time. I can make my son understand almost anything about the house, but I have found it impossible to explain the plan of salvation to him. Perhaps his sister can make him see it. She is visiting from Sherman. She is in the garden."

The group walked out into the garden. "Sister," spoke Nelson, "Bud here wants to come into the church. We want to know if he understands the step he contemplates. Can you ask him some questions about Jesus Christ for us and make him understand?"

"Brother Nelson," said the sister, "I am twenty- seven years old. I have been a Christian and a church-member since I was eight. Ever since I was a little girl, I have brought picture cards from Sunday school for Bud. I've tried every way I know how to make him know about the Saviour, but it just is no use. He doesn't seem to understand. Don't you reckon the Lord will take care of him anyway?"

"I do not know, sister," said the preacher, "but let's ask Him. Let us pray." The six of them got down on their knees in the garden. One by one the five normal ones lifted their voices to God for the boy's soul. They then separated to their tasks.

That night the brush arbor was packed. The news of Bud's problem had been broadcast over the countryside. Skaggs led the song service. Oby Nelson preached. When he gave the invitation, the first man to walk down the aisle was Bud Walker. Nelson bowed his head in his hands and sobbed. The problem was beyond him. Bud knelt in front of the pulpit. A deathly silence, broken only by muffled sobs, settled on the crowd. After some minutes the preacher felt a tug at his coat. Bud, his face lit up with an unearthly light, stood before him. The boy did not offer his hand as was the custom. Instead, he raised his two hands and moved his arms as though he were embracing the skies, then brought his hands down to his heart. He repeated the gesture touching the Bible, touched his dusty knees, stretched out his hand to the preacher, and everybody in the crowd knew that Jesus had worked one more miracle and saved the deaf and dumb boy's soul.

Facing that Baptist Association crowd in Navarro County, Texas, Nelson finished his story. "Brethren and sisters," he said, "Bud Walker won more souls to Christ during the remainder of that revival than any three of us."

When the service was over and we all were out in the church yard, eating our dinner, I questioned Oby further.

"Oby, that surely was a great story, but boy, didn't you stretch it a little at the end?"

"What do you mean, stretch it a little?"

"Well, how could a deaf and dumb person lead souls to Christ?"

"That's all you know," said Oby. "Put your plate and cup down." I did, on the running-board of a near-by car. Oby did the same. He came up to me, put his arm around my shoulder, and spoke on.

"After the night of his decision, Bud would do personal work in that crowd. He'd go up to an unsaved man or boy, put his arm about him, press him a little, point to that one's heart, point to his own heart, point to the heavens, point down the aisle, and gently compel them to the front."

Nelson and I left our lunches just where they were. We walked over to a barn almost filled with hay, burrowed into it, stretched out on our faces, and held a prayer-meeting. I do not know what Oby said. I was too busy getting right with Jesus about that time. When my friend had finished his prayer, I lifted my heart and voice to God, and this is what I said:

"Lord Jesus, it is not in me to be a Paul. It is not in me to be a Wesley. It is not in me to be a Truett. But, oh, make me, oh, do make me a Bud Walker. Let me use what You have given me for Your glory and the salvation of souls."

* * *

WHO IS THE "GREATEST" PREACHER?

There is a beautiful story in the biography of Dr. G. Campbell Morgan. He has four sons, and they are all preachers. His youngest son, Howard, took his father's place on the other side of the Atlantic when Dr. Morgan came to London, and Howard is considered to be a great preacher. Someone once came into the drawing-room when all the family were there. They thought they would see what Howard was made of, and they asked him this question, "Howard, who is the greatest preacher in your family?" Howard has a great admiration for his father, and he looked straight across at him, and then, without a moment's hesitation, he answered, "Mother!" *Some of those who have never stood on platforms or in pulpits are preaching the greatest sermons!* —A. LINDSAY GLEGG, in *Youth With A Capital Why.*

* * *

WORKS, 1

A young lady and gentleman came into a drug store accompanied by an elderly gentleman, the father of the young woman. On entering the store they saw a weighing machine. The lady said to her father, "Step up on the machine, father, and see how much you weigh."

She then left him and went to the counter to give an

order. The old gentleman stepped on the machine. Soon his daughter returned and said, "Well, father, how much do you weigh?"

"I don't know," replied the father.

"Didn't you see the hand spin round and the finger rest on a certain number?" asked the daughter.

"No," he replied.

The daughter then shook the machine, but still the indicating hand did not move. The machine was a beautiful piece of mechanism; the face of the dial was elaborately painted and designed, but it did not indicate the man's weight. "That's strange," said the daughter, "did you put a penny in the slot, Papa?"

"Why, no," answered the man.

"Oh, then," said the daughter, "that's the reason it doesn't work; you have to put a penny in the slot."

* * *

WORKS, 2

An old colored preacher was convalescing from a severe illness. His appetite was returning. He longed for a piece of chicken. So he prayed, "O Lord, please send me a chicken."

Alas, no chicken came. The craving for a piece of good, old-fashioned fried chicken was increasing. But the prayer was not answered — no chicken was forthcoming. The preacher then changed the form of his prayer, and said, "Dear Lord, send me out after the chicken." Needless to say the preacher had fried chicken that night for supper.

* * *

WORSHIP

Do you remember the story of Rabia's pilgrimage to Mecca? Rabia joined a caravan of pilgrims. She crossed the sea; she crossed the desert. Night brightened into day and day faded into night, forty, fifty, sixty times, until at last they came, with crowds of other worshippers, to the sacred city. There Rabia bent in worship at the shrine, to learn what the Samaritan woman learned beneath the shadow of Gerizim. "Neither in this city, nor yet at Jerusalem, shall ye worship the Father." And Rabia arose, and returned wiser to her home, saying:

Thou fool to tread the desert road,
To toss upon the dreary sea,
To come so far to seek thy God,
Who always was so near to thee.

OUTLINES INDEXED BY TITLE

OUTLINES INDEXED BY TEXT

ILLUSTRATIONS INDEXED BY TITLE

ILLUSTRATIONS INDEXED BY TEXT

Printed in the United States of America

NOTES

NOTES